THE PSALMS | for Today

Today's English Version

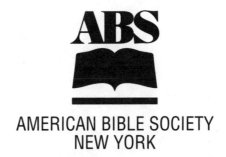

ABS

AMERICAN BIBLE SOCIETY
NEW YORK

THE PSALMS
in Today's English Version

This is a Portion of Holy Scripture in Today's English Version from the *Good News Bible*. The American Bible Society is a not-for-profit organization which publishes Scriptures without doctrinal note or comment. Since 1816, its single mission has been to make the Word of God easily available to people everywhere at the lowest possible cost and in the languages they understand best. Working toward this goal, the ABS is a member of the United Bible Societies, a worldwide effort that extends to more than 180 countries and territories. You are urged to read the Bible and to share it with others. For a catalog of Scripture publications, write to the American Bible Society, 1865 Broadway, New York, N.Y. 10023.

Printed in the United States of America
Eng. Port. TEV590P-100792
ABS-6/00-3,000-290,000—RRD6(23)

PREFACE

This translation of *The Psalms* attempts to represent the meaning of the Hebrew text as faithfully as possible, and at the same time convey something of the grace and beauty of the original poetry. The basic poetic structure of the Psalms consists of a statement which is repeated, in a modified fashion, in the next line. Sometimes this parallelism is continued over several lines. The possible variations are almost unlimited, and the reader who is aware of them will discover new beauty in the Psalms. In addition, unusual words and figurative expressions help create and sustain a poetic atmosphere.

Ancient Hebrew poetry did not have rhyme, and the meter was quite different from what is commonly used in English. This translation has been made in free verse, and the translators have tried to put the Psalms in easy-flowing, rhythmical lines that can be effective in public worship as well as in private devotion.

Today's English Version is a distinctive translation, which does not conform to traditional vocabulary or style. It seeks instead to express the meaning of the Hebrew text in words and forms accepted as standard by people everywhere who employ English as a means of communication.

Where there is general agreement that the Hebrew text presents unresolved difficulties in interpretation, this translation employs the evidence of other ancient texts or follows present-day scholarly consensus. All such modifications are identified in footnotes. Other footnotes give information designed to help the reader understand the meaning of the text, especially where ancient beliefs or customs are expressed or alluded to.

The Bible in Today's English Version is called the *Good News Bible* and is available from the American Bible Society.

PSALMS

Introduction

The book of *Psalms* is the hymnbook and prayer book of the Bible. Composed by different authors over a long period of time, these hymns and prayers were collected and used by the people of Israel in their worship, and eventually this collection was included in their Scriptures.

These religious poems are of many kinds: there are hymns of praise and worship of God; prayers for help, protection, and salvation; pleas for forgiveness; songs of thanksgiving for God's blessings; and petitions for the punishment of enemies. These prayers are both personal and national; some portray the most intimate feelings of one person, while others represent the needs and feelings of all the people of God.

The psalms were used by Jesus, quoted by the writers of the New Testament, and became the treasured book of worship of the Christian Church from its beginning.

Outline of Contents

The 150 psalms are grouped into five collections, or books, as follows:

BOOK ONE
(Psalms 1–41)

True Happiness

1 Happy are those
who reject the advice of evil people,
who do not follow the example of sinners
or join those who have no use for God.
2 Instead, they find joy in obeying the Law of
the LORD,
and they study it day and night.
3 They are like trees that grow beside a stream,
that bear fruit at the right time,
and whose leaves do not dry up.
They succeed in everything they do.

4 But evil people are not like this at all;
they are like straw that the wind blows
away.
5 Sinners will be condemned by God
and kept apart from God's own people.
6 The righteous are guided and protected by the
LORD,
but the evil are on the way to their doom.

God's Chosen King

2 Why do the nations plan rebellion?
Why do people make their useless plots?
2 Their kings revolt,
their rulers plot together against the LORD
and against the king he chose.

3 "Let us free ourselves from their rule,"
     they say;
   "let us throw off their control."

4 From his throne in heaven the Lord laughs
     and mocks their feeble plans.
5 Then he warns them in anger
     and terrifies them with his fury.
6 "On Zion,a my sacred hill," he says,
   "I have installed my king."

7 "I will announce," says the king, "what the
     LORD has declared.
   He said to me: 'You are my son;
   today I have become your father.
8 Ask, and I will give you all the nations;
   the whole earth will be yours.
9 You will break them with an iron rod;
     you will shatter them in pieces like a
        clay pot.' "

10 Now listen to this warning, you kings;
     learn this lesson, you rulers of the world:
11 Serve the LORD with fear;
     tremble 12 and bow down to him; b
   or else his anger will be quickly aroused,
     and you will suddenly die.
   Happy are all who go to him for protection.

a ZION: *The term "Zion" (originally a designation for "David's City," the Jebusite stronghold captured by King David's forces) was later extended in meaning to refer to the hill on which the Temple stood.* b Probable text tremble . . . him; *some other possible texts* with trembling kiss his feet *and* with trembling kiss the Son *and* tremble and kiss the mighty one; *Hebrew unclear.*

Morning Prayer for Help [c]

3 I have so many enemies, LORD,
  so many who turn against me!
2 They talk about me and say,
  "God will not help him."

3 But you, O LORD, are always my shield from
    danger;
  you give me victory
  and restore my courage.
4 I call to the LORD for help,
  and from his sacred hill[d] he answers me.

5 I lie down and sleep,
  and all night long the LORD protects me.
6 I am not afraid of the thousands of enemies
  who surround me on every side.

7 Come, LORD! Save me, my God!
  You punish all my enemies
  and leave them powerless to harm me.
8 Victory comes from the LORD—
  may he bless his people.

Evening Prayer for Help [e]

4 Answer me when I pray,
  O God, my defender!
When I was in trouble, you helped me.
  Be kind to me now and hear my prayer.

---

[c] HEBREW TITLE: *A psalm by David, after he ran away from his son Absalom.*
[d] SACRED HILL: *See 2.6.*   [e] HEBREW TITLE: *A psalm by David.*

2 How long will you people insult me?
    How long will you love what is worthless
    and go after what is false?

3 Remember that the LORD has chosen the
      righteous for his own,
    and he hears me when I call to him.

4 Tremble with fear and stop sinning;
    think deeply about this,
    when you lie in silence on your beds.
5 Offer the right sacrifices to the LORD,
    and put your trust in him.

6 There are many who pray:
    "Give us more blessings, O LORD.
    Look on us with kindness!"
7 But the joy that you have given me
    is more than they will ever have
    with all their grain and wine.

8 When I lie down, I go to sleep in peace;
    you alone, O LORD, keep me perfectly safe.

A Prayer for Protection *e*

5 Listen to my words, O LORD,
    and hear my sighs.
2 Listen to my cry for help,
    my God and king!

    I pray to you, O LORD;

e HEBREW TITLE: *A psalm by David.*

3   you hear my voice in the morning;
   at sunrise I offer my prayer*ᶠ*
    and wait for your answer.

4 You are not a God who is pleased with
      wrongdoing;
   you allow no evil in your presence.
5 You cannot stand the sight of the proud;
   you hate all wicked people.
6 You destroy all liars
   and despise violent, deceitful people.

7 But because of your great love
   I can come into your house;
 I can worship in your holy Temple
   and bow down to you in reverence.
8 LORD, I have so many enemies!
   Lead me to do your will;
   make your way plain for me to follow.

9 What my enemies say can never be trusted;
   they only want to destroy.
 Their words are flattering and smooth,
   but full of deadly deceit.
10 Condemn and punish them, O God;
   may their own plots cause their ruin.
 Drive them out of your presence
   because of their many sins
   and their rebellion against you.

11 But all who find safety in you will rejoice;

ᶠ prayer; or sacrifice.

they can always sing for joy.
Protect those who love you;
    because of you they are truly happy.
12 You bless those who obey you, LORD;
    your love protects them like a shield.

A Prayer for Help in Time of Trouble [g]

6 LORD, don't be angry and rebuke me!
        Don't punish me in your anger!
2 I am worn out, O LORD; have pity on me!
    Give me strength; I am completely
        exhausted
3   and my whole being is deeply troubled.
    How long, O LORD, will you wait to help me?

4 Come and save me, LORD;
    in your mercy rescue me from death.
5 In the world of the dead you are not
        remembered;
    no one can praise you there.

6 I am worn out with grief;
    every night my bed is damp from my
        weeping;
    my pillow is soaked with tears.
7 I can hardly see;
    my eyes are so swollen
    from the weeping caused by my enemies.

8 Keep away from me, you evil people!
    The LORD hears my weeping;

g HEBREW TITLE: *A psalm by David.*

⁹   he listens to my cry for help
    and will answer my prayer.
¹⁰ My enemies will know the bitter shame of
    defeat;
    in sudden confusion they will be driven
    away.

A Prayer for Justice *h*

7   O Lᴏʀᴅ, my God, I come to you for
    protection;
    rescue me and save me from all who
    pursue me,
² or else like a lion they will carry me off
    where no one can save me,
    and there they will tear me to pieces.

³⁻⁴ O Lᴏʀᴅ, my God, if I have wronged anyone,
    if I have betrayed a friend
    or without cause done violence to my
    enemy*i*—
    if I have done any of these things—
⁵ then let my enemies pursue me and catch me,
    let them cut me down and kill me
    and leave me lifeless on the ground!

⁶ Rise in your anger, O Lᴏʀᴅ!
    Stand up against the fury of my enemies;
    rouse yourself and help me!
Justice is what you demand,

---

h Hᴇʙʀᴇᴡ ᴛɪᴛʟᴇ: *A song which David sang to the Lᴏʀᴅ because of Cush the Benjaminite.*
i without cause done violence to my enemy; *or* shown mercy to someone who wronged me unjustly.

7   so bring together all the peoples
           around you,
       and rule over them from above.^j
8 You are the judge of all people.
       Judge in my favor, O LORD;
       you know that I am innocent.
9 You are a righteous God
       and judge our thoughts and desires.
   Stop the wickedness of evildoers
       and reward those who are good.

10 God is my protector;
       he saves those who obey him.
11 God is a righteous judge
       and always condemns the wicked.
12 If they do not change their ways,
       God will sharpen his sword.
   He bends his bow and makes it ready;
13   he takes up his deadly weapons
       and aims his burning arrows.

14 See how wicked people think up evil;
       they plan trouble and practice deception.
15 But in the traps they set for others,
       they themselves get caught.
16 So they are punished by their own evil
       and are hurt by their own violence.

17 I thank the LORD for his justice;
       I sing praises to the LORD, the Most High.

^j *Probable text* rule over them from above; *Hebrew* return above over them.

God's Glory and Human Dignity [k]

8 O Lord, our Lord,
  your greatness is seen in all the world!
Your praise reaches up to the heavens;
2   it is sung by children and babies.
You are safe and secure from all your
      enemies;
   you stop anyone who opposes you.

3 When I look at the sky, which you have
      made,
   at the moon and the stars, which you set in
      their places—
4 what are human beings, that you think of
      them;
   mere mortals, that you care for them?

5 Yet you made them inferior only to
      yourself; [l]
   you crowned them with glory and honor.
6 You appointed them rulers over everything
      you made;
   you placed them over all creation:
7   sheep and cattle, and the wild animals too;
8   the birds and the fish
   and the creatures in the seas.

9 O Lord, our Lord,
   your greatness is seen in all the world!

k HEBREW TITLE: *A psalm by David.*   l yourself; *or* the gods, *or* the angels.

11/21

Jeanette,

I had to give this to you in a brown paper bag because this is embarrassing! (Don't laugh!!) I ordered these books of Psalms from a catalog because they were so cheap. A friend of mine told me she was reading the Psalms for comfort after the disaster & I thought of what you said about how you & Mike were looking for comfort from God/church. Anyway, this is clearly the geriatric edition, but oh well, you may as well have it. At least you won't need your glasses to read it!

In case you are interested in going to Willow Creek for Christmas, I have enclosed the ticket (they are free) instructions. You are certainly welcome to come with me & my family. The satellite church that will be starting near you will eventually meet at the Wheaton-Warrenville High School on Sunday mornings at nine. Apparently the building is not available yet. I'll let you know.

Hope you have a great Thanksgiving.

Jeanie

Thanksgiving to God for His Justice [m]

9 I will praise you, LORD, with all my heart;
I will tell of all the wonderful things you
have done.
2 I will sing with joy because of you.
I will sing praise to you, Almighty God.

3 My enemies turn back when you appear;
they fall down and die.
4 You are fair and honest in your judgments,
and you have judged in my favor.

5 You have condemned the heathen
and destroyed the wicked;
they will be remembered no more.
6 Our enemies are finished forever;
you have destroyed their cities,
and they are completely forgotten.

7 But the LORD is king forever;
he has set up his throne for judgment.
8 He rules the world with righteousness;
he judges the nations with justice.

9 The LORD is a refuge for the oppressed,
a place of safety in times of trouble.
10 Those who know you, LORD, will trust you;
you do not abandon anyone who comes
to you.

11 Sing praise to the LORD, who rules in Zion!

[m] HEBREW TITLE: *A psalm by David.*

Tell every nation what he has done!
12 God remembers those who suffer;
　　he does not forget their cry,
　　and he punishes those who wrong them.

13 Be merciful to me, O LORD!
　　See the sufferings my enemies cause me!
　Rescue me from death, O LORD,
14　　that I may stand before the people of
　　　　Jerusalem
　　and tell them all the things for which I
　　　　praise you.
　I will rejoice because you saved me.

15 The heathen have dug a pit and fallen in;
　　they have been caught in their own trap.
16 The LORD has revealed himself by his
　　　　righteous judgments,
　　and the wicked are trapped by their own
　　　　deeds.

17 Death is the destiny of all the wicked,
　　of all those who reject God.
18 The needy will not always be neglected;
　　the hope of the poor will not be crushed
　　　　forever.

19 Come, LORD! Do not let anyone defy you!
　　Bring the heathen before you
　　and pronounce judgment on them.
20 Make them afraid, O LORD;
　　make them know that they are only mortal
　　　　beings.

A Prayer for Justice

10 Why are you so far away, O LORD?
Why do you hide yourself when we are
in trouble?

2 The wicked are proud and persecute the poor;
catch them in the traps they have made.

3 The wicked are proud of their evil desires;
the greedy curse and reject the LORD.
4 The wicked do not care about the LORD;
in their pride they think that God doesn't
matter.

5 The wicked succeed in everything.
They cannot understand God's judgments;
they sneer at their enemies.
6 They say to themselves, "We will never fail;
we will never be in trouble."
7 Their speech is filled with curses, lies, and
threats;
they are quick to speak hateful, evil words.

8 They hide themselves in the villages,
waiting to murder innocent people.
They spy on their helpless victims;
9   they wait in their hiding place like lions.
They lie in wait for the poor;
they catch them in their traps and drag
them away.

10 The helpless victims lie crushed;
brute strength has defeated them.

11 The wicked say to themselves, "God doesn't
      care!
    He has closed his eyes and will never
      see me!"

12 O LORD, punish those wicked people!
    Remember those who are suffering!
13 How can the wicked despise God
    and say to themselves, "He will not
      punish me"?

14 But you do see; you take notice of trouble
      and suffering
    and are always ready to help.
  The helpless commit themselves to you;
    you have always helped the needy.

15 Break the power of wicked and evil people;
    punish them for the wrong they have done
    until they do it no more.

16 The LORD is king forever and ever.
    Those who worship other gods
    will vanish from his land.

17 You will listen, O LORD, to the prayers of the
      lowly;
    you will give them courage.
18 You will hear the cries of the oppressed and
      the orphans;
    you will judge in their favor,
    so that mortal men may cause terror no
      more.

Confidence in the LORD [n]

11   I trust in the LORD for safety.
How foolish of you to say to me,
"Fly away like a bird to the mountains,[o]
2   because the wicked have drawn their bows
and aimed their arrows
to shoot from the shadows at good people.
3 There is nothing a good person can do
when everything falls apart."

4 The LORD is in his holy temple;
he has his throne in heaven.
He watches people everywhere
and knows what they are doing.
5 He examines the good and the wicked alike;
the lawless he hates with all his heart.

6 He sends down flaming coals[p] and burning
sulfur on the wicked;
he punishes them with scorching winds.
7 The LORD is righteous and loves good deeds;
those who do them will live in his presence.

A Prayer for Help [q]

12   Help us, LORD!
There is not a good person left;
honest people can no longer be found.
2 All of them lie to one another;
they deceive each other with flattery.

---

[n] HEBREW TITLE: *By David.*   [o] *Some ancient translations* like a bird to the mountains; *Hebrew* bird, to your *(plural)* mountain.   [p] *One ancient translation* coals; *Hebrew* traps.   [q] HEBREW TITLE: *A psalm by David.*

3 Silence those flattering tongues, O Lord!
    Close those boastful mouths that say,
4 "With our words we get what we want.
    We will say what we wish,
    and no one can stop us."

5 "But now I will come," says the Lord,
    "because the needy are oppressed
    and the persecuted groan in pain.
I will give them the security they long for."

6 The promises of the Lord can be trusted;
    they are as genuine as silver
    refined seven times in the furnace.

7-8 The wicked are everywhere,
    and everyone praises what is evil.
Keep us always safe, O Lord,
    and preserve us from such people.

A Prayer for Help *q*

13 How much longer will you forget me,
        Lord? Forever?
    How much longer will you hide yourself
        from me?
2 How long must I endure trouble?
    How long will sorrow fill my heart day and
        night?
    How long will my enemies triumph
        over me?

q HEBREW TITLE: *A psalm by David.*

³ Look at me, O Lord my God, and
        answer me.
    Restore my strength; don't let me die.
⁴ Don't let my enemies say, "We have
        defeated him."
    Don't let them gloat over my downfall.

⁵ I rely on your constant love;
    I will be glad, because you will rescue me.
⁶ I will sing to you, O Lord,
    because you have been good to me.

Human Wickedness ʳ
(Psalm 53)

14 Fools say to themselves,
        "There is no God!"
    They are all corrupt,
        and they have done terrible things;
        there is no one who does what is right.

² The Lord looks down from heaven at us
        humans
        to see if there are any who are wise,
        any who worship him.
³ But they have all gone wrong;
        they are all equally bad.
    Not one of them does what is right,
        not a single one.

⁴ "Don't they know?" asks the Lord.
    "Are all these evildoers ignorant?

ʳ HEBREW TITLE: *By David.*

They live by robbing my people,
and they never pray to me."

5 But then they will be terrified,
for God is with those who obey him.
6 Evildoers frustrate the plans of the humble,
but the LORD is their protection.

7 How I pray that victory
will come to Israel from Zion.
How happy the people of Israel will be
when the LORD makes them prosperous
again!

What God Requires [s]

15 LORD, who may enter your Temple?
Who may worship on Zion, your sacred
hill?[t]

2 Those who obey God in everything
and always do what is right,
whose words are true and sincere,
3   and who do not slander others.
They do no wrong to their friends
nor spread rumors about their neighbors.
4 They despise those whom God rejects,
but honor those who obey the LORD.
They always do what they promise,
no matter how much it may cost.
5 They make loans without charging interest

s HEBREW TITLE: *A psalm by David.*   t SACRED HILL: *See 2.6.*

and cannot be bribed to testify against the
    innocent.

Whoever does these things will always be
    secure.

A Prayer of Confidence[u]

16 Protect me, O God; I trust in you for
    safety.
2 I say to the LORD, "You are my Lord;
    all the good things I have come from you."

3 How excellent are the LORD's faithful people!
    My greatest pleasure is to be with them.

4 Those who rush to other gods
    bring many troubles on themselves.[v]
I will not take part in their sacrifices;
    I will not worship their gods.

5 You, LORD, are all I have,
    and you give me all I need;
    my future is in your hands.
6 How wonderful are your gifts to me;
    how good they are!

7 I praise the LORD, because he guides me,
    and in the night my conscience warns me.
8 I am always aware of the LORD's presence;
    he is near, and nothing can shake me.

[u] HEBREW TITLE: *A psalm by David.*   [v] *Probable text* Those . . . themselves; *Hebrew unclear.*

9 And so I am thankful and glad,
   and I feel completely secure,
10 because you protect me from the power of
     death.
I have served you faithfully,
   and you will not abandon me to the world
     of the dead.

11 You will show me the path that leads to life;
   your presence fills me with joy
   and brings me pleasure forever.

The Prayer of an Innocent Person w

17   Listen, O LORD, to my plea for justice;
     pay attention to my cry for help!
Listen to my honest prayer.
2 You will judge in my favor,
   because you know what is right.

3 You know my heart.
   You have come to me at night;
   you have examined me completely
   and found no evil desire in me.
I speak no evil, 4 as others do;
   I have obeyed your command
   and have not followed paths of violence.
5 I have always walked in your way
   and have never strayed from it.

w HEBREW TITLE: *A prayer by David.*

⁶ I pray to you, O God, because you
   answer me;
  so turn to me and listen to my words.
⁷ Reveal your wonderful love and save me;
  at your side I am safe from my enemies.

⁸ Protect me as you would your very eyes;
  hide me in the shadow of your wings
⁹ from the attacks of the wicked.

 Deadly enemies surround me;
¹⁰ they have no pity and speak proudly.
¹¹ They are around me now, wherever I turn,
  watching for a chance to pull me down.
¹² They are like lions, waiting for me,
  wanting to tear me to pieces.

¹³ Come, LORD! Oppose my enemies and defeat
   them!
 Save me from the wicked by your sword;
¹⁴ save me from those who in this life have all
   they want.
 Punish them with the sufferings you have
   stored up for them;
  may there be enough for their children
  and some left over for their children's
   children!

¹⁵ But I will see you, because I have done no
   wrong;
  and when I awake, your presence will fill
   me with joy.

David's Song of Victory [x]
(2 Samuel 22.1-51)

18 How I love you, LORD!
You are my defender.

2 The LORD is my protector;
   he is my strong fortress.
My God is my protection,
   and with him I am safe.
He protects me like a shield;
   he defends me and keeps me safe.
3 I call to the LORD,
   and he saves me from my enemies.
Praise the LORD!

4 The danger of death was all around me;
   the waves of destruction rolled over me.
5 The danger of death was around me,
   and the grave set its trap for me.
6 In my trouble I called to the LORD;
   I called to my God for help.
In his temple he heard my voice;
   he listened to my cry for help.

7 Then the earth trembled and shook;
   the foundations of the mountains rocked
      and quivered,
   because God was angry.
8 Smoke poured out of his nostrils,
   a consuming flame and burning coals from
      his mouth.

x HEBREW TITLE: *The words that David, the LORD's servant, sang to the LORD on the day the LORD saved him from Saul and all his other enemies.*

9 He tore the sky open and came down
    with a dark cloud under his feet.
10 He flew swiftly on his winged creature;*y*
    he traveled on the wings of the wind.
11 He covered himself with darkness;
    thick clouds, full of water, surrounded him.
12 Hailstones and flashes of fire
    came from the lightning before him
    and broke through the dark clouds.

13 Then the LORD thundered from the sky;
    and the voice of the Most High was
        heard.*z*
14 He shot his arrows and scattered his enemies;
    with flashes of lightning he sent them
        running.
15 The floor of the ocean was laid bare,
    and the foundations of the earth were
        uncovered,
  when you rebuked your enemies, LORD,
    and roared at them in anger.

16 The LORD reached down from above and took
        hold of me;
    he pulled me out of the deep waters.
17 He rescued me from my powerful enemies
    and from all those who hate me—
    they were too strong for me.
18 When I was in trouble, they attacked me,
    but the LORD protected me.
19 He helped me out of danger;

y WINGED CREATURE: *See Word List.*   *z One ancient translation (and see 2 S 22.14) was*
heard; *Hebrew* was heard hailstones and flashes of fire.

he saved me because he was pleased
    with me.

20 The LORD rewards me because I do what is
      right;
    he blesses me because I am innocent.
21 I have obeyed the law of the LORD;
    I have not turned away from my God.
22 I have observed all his laws;
    I have not disobeyed his commands.
23 He knows that I am faultless,
    that I have kept myself from doing wrong.
24 And so he rewards me because I do what is
      right,
    because he knows that I am innocent.

25 O LORD, you are faithful to those who are
      faithful to you;
    completely good to those who are perfect.
26 You are pure to those who are pure,
    but hostile to those who are wicked.
27 You save those who are humble,
    but you humble those who are proud.

28 O LORD, you give me light;
    you dispel my darkness.
29 You give me strength to attack my enemies
    and power to overcome their defenses.

30 This God—how perfect are his deeds!
    How dependable his words!
  He is like a shield
    for all who seek his protection.

31 The LORD alone is God;
    God alone is our defense.
32 He is the God who makes me strong,
    who makes my pathway safe.
33 He makes me sure-footed as a deer;
    he keeps me safe on the mountains.
34 He trains me for battle,
    so that I can use the strongest bow.

35 O LORD, you protect me and save me;
    your care has made me great,
    and your power has kept me safe.
36 You have kept me from being captured,
    and I have never fallen.
37 I pursue my enemies and catch them;
    I do not stop until I destroy them.
38 I strike them down, and they cannot rise;
    they lie defeated before me.
39 You give me strength for the battle
    and victory over my enemies.
40 You make my enemies run from me;
    I destroy those who hate me.
41 They cry for help, but no one saves them;
    they call to the LORD, but he does not
      answer.
42 I crush them, so that they become like dust
    which the wind blows away.
  I trample on them like mud in the streets.

43 You saved me from a rebellious people
    and made me ruler over the nations;
    people I did not know have now become
      my subjects.

44 Foreigners bow before me;
     when they hear me, they obey.
45 They lose their courage
     and come trembling from their fortresses.

46 The LORD lives! Praise my defender!
     Proclaim the greatness of the God who
          saves me.
47 He gives me victory over my enemies;
     he subdues the nations under me
48   and saves me from my foes.

O LORD, you give me victory over my
          enemies
     and protect me from violent people.
49 And so I praise you among the nations;
     I sing praises to you.

50 God gives great victories to his king;
     he shows constant love to the one he has
          chosen,
     to David and his descendants forever.

God's Glory in Creation [a]

19 How clearly the sky reveals God's glory!
     How plainly it shows what he has done!
2 Each day announces it to the following day;
     each night repeats it to the next.
3 No speech or words are used,
     no sound is heard;
4 yet their message [b] goes out to all the world

[a] HEBREW TITLE: *A psalm by David.*   [b] *Some ancient translations* message; *Hebrew* line.

and is heard to the ends of the earth.
God made a home in the sky for the sun;
5   it comes out in the morning like a happy
        bridegroom,
    like an athlete eager to run a race.
6 It starts at one end of the sky
    and goes across to the other.
    Nothing can hide from its heat.

The Law of the LORD

7 The law of the LORD is perfect;
    it gives new strength.
The commands of the LORD are trustworthy,
    giving wisdom to those who lack it.
8 The laws of the LORD are right,
    and those who obey them are happy.
The commands of the LORD are just
    and give understanding to the mind.
9 Reverence for the LORD is good;
    it will continue forever.
The judgments of the LORD are just;
    they are always fair.
10 They are more desirable than the finest gold;
    they are sweeter than the purest honey.
11 They give knowledge to me, your servant;
    I am rewarded for obeying them.

12 None of us can see our own errors;
    deliver me, LORD, from hidden faults!
13 Keep me safe, also, from willful sins;
    don't let them rule over me.
Then I shall be perfect

and free from the evil of sin.

14 May my words and my thoughts be
      acceptable to you,
   O LORD, my refuge and my redeemer!

A Prayer for Victory *c*

20 May the LORD answer you when you are
         in trouble!
   May the God of Jacob protect you!
2 May he send you help from his Temple
      and give you aid from Mount Zion.
3 May he accept all your offerings
      and be pleased with all your sacrifices.
4 May he give you what you desire
      and make all your plans succeed.
5 Then we will shout for joy over your victory
      and celebrate your triumph by praising
         our God.
   May the LORD answer all your requests.

6 Now I know that the LORD gives victory to
      his chosen king;
      he answers him from his holy heaven
      and by his power gives him great victories.
7 Some trust in their war chariots
      and others in their horses,
      but we trust in the power of the LORD
         our God.
8 Such people will stumble and fall,
      but we will rise and stand firm.

c HEBREW TITLE: *A psalm by David.*

9 Give victory to the king, O LORD;
    answer[d] us when we call.

Praise for Victory[e]

21 The king is glad, O LORD, because you
       gave him strength;
    he rejoices because you made him
      victorious.
2 You have given him his heart's desire;
    you have answered his request.

3 You came to him with great blessings
    and set a crown of gold on his head.
4 He asked for life, and you gave it,
    a long and lasting life.

5 His glory is great because of your help;
    you have given him fame and majesty.
6 Your blessings are with him forever,
    and your presence fills him with joy.

7 The king trusts in the LORD Almighty;
    and because of the LORD's constant love
    he will always be secure.
8 The king will capture all his enemies;
    he will capture everyone who hates him.
9 He will destroy them like a blazing fire
    when he appears.

The LORD will devour them in his anger,
    and fire will consume them.

---

[d] *Some ancient translations* answer; *Hebrew* he will answer.   [e] HEBREW TITLE: *A psalm by David.*

¹⁰ None of their descendants will survive;
     the king will kill them all.

¹¹ They make their plans, and plot against him,
     but they will not succeed.
¹² He will shoot his arrows at them
     and make them turn and run.

¹³ We praise you, LORD, for your great strength!
     We will sing and praise your power.

A Cry of Anguish and a Song of Praise [e]

22 My God, my God, why have you
          abandoned me?
   I have cried desperately for help,
     but still it does not come.
² During the day I call to you, my God,
     but you do not answer;
   I call at night,
     but get no rest.
³ But you are enthroned as the Holy One,
     the one whom Israel praises.
⁴ Our ancestors put their trust in you;
     they trusted you, and you saved them.
⁵ They called to you and escaped from danger;
     they trusted you and were not disappointed.

⁶ But I am no longer a human being; I am a
          worm,
     despised and scorned by everyone!
⁷ All who see me make fun of me;

[e] HEBREW TITLE: *A psalm by David.*

they stick out their tongues and shake their
    heads.
8 "You relied on the LORD," they say.
  "Why doesn't he save you?
 If the LORD likes you,
  why doesn't he help you?"

9 It was you who brought me safely through
    birth,
  and when I was a baby, you kept me safe.
10 I have relied on you since the day I was born,
  and you have always been my God.
11 Do not stay away from me!
  Trouble is near,
  and there is no one to help.

12 Many enemies surround me like bulls;
  they are all around me,
  like fierce bulls from the land of Bashan.
13 They open their mouths like lions,
  roaring and tearing at me.

14 My strength is gone,
  gone like water spilled on the ground.
 All my bones are out of joint;
  my heart is like melted wax.
15 My throat *f* is as dry as dust,
  and my tongue sticks to the roof of my
    mouth.
 You have left me for dead in the dust.

f Probable text throat; *Hebrew* strength.

16 An evil gang is around me;
    like a pack of dogs they close in on me;
    they tear at*g* my hands and feet.
17 All my bones can be seen.
    My enemies look at me and stare.
18 They gamble for my clothes
    and divide them among themselves.

19 O LORD, don't stay away from me!
    Come quickly to my rescue!
20 Save me from the sword;
    save my life from these dogs.
21 Rescue me from these lions;
    I am helpless *h* before these wild bulls.

22 I will tell my people what you have done;
    I will praise you in their assembly:
23 "Praise him, you servants of the LORD!
    Honor him, you descendants of Jacob!
    Worship him, you people of Israel!
24 He does not neglect the poor or ignore their
        suffering;
    he does not turn away from them,
    but answers when they call for help."

25 In the full assembly I will praise you for what
        you have done;
    in the presence of those who worship you
    I will offer the sacrifices I promised.
26 The poor will eat as much as they want;

g Some ancient translations they tear at; *others* they tie; *Hebrew* like a lion.
h Some ancient translations I am helpless; *Hebrew* you answered me.

those who come to the LORD will
   praise him.
May they prosper forever!

27 All nations will remember the LORD.
   From every part of the world they will turn
     to him;
   all races will worship him.
28 The LORD is king,
   and he rules the nations.

29 All proud people will bow down to him; *i*
   all mortals will bow down before him.
30 Future generations will serve him;
   they will speak of the Lord to the coming
     generation.
31 People not yet born will be told:
   "The Lord saved his people."

The LORD Our Shepherd *j*

23 The LORD is my shepherd;
   I have everything I need.
2 He lets me rest in fields of green grass
   and leads me to quiet pools of fresh water.
3 He gives me new strength.
He guides me in the right paths,
   as he has promised.
4 Even if I go through the deepest darkness,
   I will not be afraid, LORD,
   for you are with me.
Your shepherd's rod and staff protect me.

i Probable text will bow down to him; *Hebrew* will eat and bow down.
j HEBREW TITLE: *A psalm by David.*

5 You prepare a banquet for me,
    where all my enemies can see me;
  you welcome me as an honored guest
    and fill my cup to the brim.
6 I know that your goodness and love will be
        with me all my life;
    and your house will be my home as long as
        I live.

The Great King*j*

24 The world and all that is in it belong to
        the LORD;
  the earth and all who live on it are his.
2 He built it on the deep waters beneath the
        earth
    and laid its foundations in the ocean depths.

3 Who has the right to go up the LORD's hill?*k*
    Who may enter his holy Temple?
4 Those who are pure in act and in thought,
    who do not worship idols
    or make false promises.
5 The LORD will bless them and save them;
    God will declare them innocent.
6 Such are the people who come to God,
    who come into the presence of the God of
        Jacob.

7 Fling wide the gates,
    open the ancient doors,
    and the great king will come in.

j HEBREW TITLE: *A psalm by David.*   *k* THE LORD'S HILL: *The hill in Jerusalem on which the Temple was built.*

8 Who is this great king?
He is the LORD, strong and mighty,
the LORD, victorious in battle.

9 Fling wide the gates,
open the ancient doors,
and the great king will come in.
10 Who is this great king?
The triumphant LORD—he is the great king!

A Prayer for Guidance and Protection[l]

25 To you, O LORD, I offer my prayer;
2   in you, my God, I trust.
Save me from the shame of defeat;
don't let my enemies gloat over me!
3 Defeat does not come to those who trust
in you,
but to those who are quick to rebel
against you.

4 Teach me your ways, O LORD;
make them known to me.
5 Teach me to live according to your truth,
for you are my God, who saves me.
I always trust in you.

6 Remember, O LORD, your kindness and
constant love
which you have shown from long ago.
7 Forgive the sins and errors of my youth.
In your constant love and goodness,

l HEBREW TITLE: By David.

remember me, LORD!

8 Because the LORD is righteous and good,
    he teaches sinners the path they should
        follow.
9 He leads the humble in the right way
    and teaches them his will.
10 With faithfulness and love he leads
    all who keep his covenant and obey his
        commands.

11 Keep your promise, LORD, and forgive my
        sins,
    for they are many.
12 Those who have reverence for the LORD
    will learn from him the path they should
        follow.
13 They will always be prosperous,
    and their children will possess the land.
14 The LORD is the friend of those who obey him
    and he affirms his covenant with them.

15 I look to the LORD for help at all times,
    and he rescues me from danger.
16 Turn to me, LORD, and be merciful to me,
    because I am lonely and weak.
17 Relieve me of my worries
    and save me from all my troubles.
18 Consider my distress and suffering
    and forgive all my sins.

19 See how many enemies I have;
    see how much they hate me.

20 Protect me and save me;
　　keep me from defeat.
　　I come to you for safety.
21 May my goodness and honesty preserve me,
　　because I trust in you.

22 From all their troubles, O God,
　　save your people Israel!

The Prayer of a Good Person[l]

26 Declare me innocent, O LORD,
　　because I do what is right
and trust you completely.
2 Examine me and test me, LORD;
　　judge my desires and thoughts.
3 Your constant love is my guide;
　　your faithfulness always leads me.[m]

4 I do not keep company with worthless people;
　　I have nothing to do with hypocrites.
5 I hate the company of the evil
　　and avoid the wicked.

6 LORD, I wash my hands to show that I am
　　　innocent
　　and march in worship around your altar.
7 I sing a hymn of thanksgiving
　　and tell of all your wonderful deeds.

8 I love the house where you live, O LORD,
　　the place where your glory dwells.

l HEBREW TITLE: *By David*.　　m your faithfulness always leads me; *or* I live in loyalty
to you.

9 Do not destroy me with the sinners;
    spare me from the fate of murderers—
10   those who do evil all the time
    and are always ready to take bribes.

11 As for me, I do what is right;
    be merciful to me and save me!

12 I am safe from all dangers;
    in the assembly of his people I praise the
      LORD.

A Prayer of Praise [n]

27 The LORD is my light and my salvation;
    I will fear no one.
The LORD protects me from all danger;
    I will never be afraid.

2 When evil people attack me and try to
      kill me,
    they stumble and fall.
3 Even if a whole army surrounds me,
    I will not be afraid;
even if enemies attack me,
    I will still trust God. [o]

4 I have asked the LORD for one thing;
    one thing only do I want:
to live in the LORD's house all my life,
    to marvel there at his goodness,
    and to ask for his guidance.

[n] HEBREW TITLE: *By David.*   [o] still trust God; *or* not lose courage.

⁵ In times of trouble he will shelter me;
    he will keep me safe in his Temple
    and make me secure on a high rock.
⁶ So I will triumph over my enemies
        around me.
    With shouts of joy I will offer sacrifices in
        his Temple;
    I will sing, I will praise the LORD.

⁷ Hear me, LORD, when I call to you!
    Be merciful and answer me!
⁸ When you said, "Come worship me,"
    I answered, "I will come, LORD."
⁹   Don't hide yourself from me!

    Don't be angry with me;
        don't turn your servant away.
    You have been my help;
        don't leave me, don't abandon me,
        O God, my savior.
¹⁰ My father and mother may abandon me,
    but the LORD will take care of me.

¹¹ Teach me, LORD, what you want me to do,
    and lead me along a safe path,
    because I have many enemies.
¹² Don't abandon me to my enemies,
    who attack me with lies and threats.

¹³ I know that I will live to see
    the LORD's goodness in this present life.
¹⁴ Trust in the LORD.

Have faith, do not despair.
Trust in the LORD.

A Prayer for Help [p]

28 O LORD, my defender, I call to you.
     Listen to my cry!
  If you do not answer me,
    I will be among those who go down to the
      world of the dead.
2 Hear me when I cry to you for help,
    when I lift my hands toward your holy
      Temple.
3 Do not condemn me with the wicked,
    with those who do evil—
    those whose words are friendly,
    but who have hatred in their hearts.

4 Punish them for what they have done,
    for the evil they have committed.
  Punish them for all their deeds;
    give them what they deserve!
5 They take no notice of what the LORD has
      done
    or of what he has made;
  so he will punish them
    and destroy them forever.

6 Give praise to the LORD;
    he has heard my cry for help.
7 The LORD protects and defends me;
    I trust in him.

[p] HEBREW TITLE: *By David.*

He gives me help and makes me glad;
I praise him with joyful songs.

8 The LORD protects his people;
he defends and saves his chosen king.
9 Save your people, LORD,
and bless those who are yours.
Be their shepherd,
and take care of them forever.

The Voice of the LORD in the Storm *q*

29 Praise the LORD, you heavenly beings;
praise his glory and power.
2 Praise the LORD's glorious name;
bow down before the Holy One when he
appears.*r*

3 The voice of the LORD is heard on the seas;
the glorious God thunders,
and his voice echoes over the ocean.
4 The voice of the LORD is heard
in all its might and majesty.

5 The voice of the LORD breaks the cedars,
even the cedars of Lebanon.
6 He makes the mountains of Lebanon jump
like calves
and makes Mount Hermon leap like a
young bull.

q HEBREW TITLE: *A psalm by David.*   *r* when he appears; *or* in garments of worship; *or*
in his beautiful Temple.

7 The voice of the LORD makes the lightning
   flash.
8 His voice makes the desert shake;
   he shakes the desert of Kadesh.
9 The LORD's voice shakes the oaks[s]
   and strips the leaves from the trees
   while everyone in his Temple shouts,
   "Glory to God!"

10 The LORD rules over the deep waters;
   he rules as king forever.
11 The LORD gives strength to his people
   and blesses them with peace.

A Prayer of Thanksgiving[t]

30 I praise you, LORD, because you have
       saved me
   and kept my enemies from gloating
       over me.
2 I cried to you for help, O LORD my God,
   and you healed me;
3   you kept me from the grave.
   I was on my way to the depths below,[u]
   but you restored my life.

4 Sing praise to the LORD,
   all his faithful people!

s Probable text shakes the oaks; Hebrew makes the deer give birth.
t HEBREW TITLE: A song for the dedication of the Temple; a psalm by David.
u THE DEPTHS BELOW: The world of the dead (see 6.5).

Remember what the Holy One has done,
  and give him thanks!
5 His anger lasts only a moment,
  his goodness for a lifetime.
Tears may flow in the night,
  but joy comes in the morning.

6 I felt secure and said to myself,
  "I will never be defeated."
7 You were good to me, LORD;
  you protected me like a mountain fortress.
But then you hid yourself from me,
  and I was afraid.

8 I called to you, LORD;
  I begged for your help:
9 "What will you gain from my death?
  What profit from my going to the grave?
Are dead people able to praise you?
  Can they proclaim your unfailing goodness?
10 Hear me, LORD, and be merciful!
  Help me, LORD!"

11 You have changed my sadness into a joyful
    dance;
  you have taken away my sorrow
  and surrounded me with joy.
12 So I will not be silent;
  I will sing praise to you.
LORD, you are my God;
  I will give you thanks forever.

A Prayer of Trust in God [v]

31 I come to you, LORD, for protection;
      never let me be defeated.
You are a righteous God;
    save me, I pray!
2 Hear me! Save me now!
Be my refuge to protect me;
    my defense to save me.

3 You are my refuge and defense;
    guide me and lead me as you have
       promised.
4 Keep me safe from the trap that has been set
     for me;
    shelter me from danger.
5 I place myself in your care.
You will save me, LORD;
    you are a faithful God.

6 You hate those who worship false gods,
    but I trust in you.
7 I will be glad and rejoice
    because of your constant love.
You see my suffering;
    you know my trouble.
8 You have not let my enemies capture me;
    you have given me freedom to go where I
     wish.

9 Be merciful to me, LORD,
    for I am in trouble;

v HEBREW TITLE: *A psalm by David.*

my eyes are tired from so much crying;
>   I am completely worn out.
10 I am exhausted by sorrow,
>   and weeping has shortened my life.
I am weak from all my troubles; w
>   even my bones are wasting away.

11 All my enemies, and especially my neighbors,
>   treat me with contempt.
Those who know me are afraid of me;
>   when they see me in the street, they run
>   away.
12 Everyone has forgotten me, as though I were
>   dead;
>   I am like something thrown away.
13 I hear many enemies whispering;
>   terror is all around me.
They are making plans against me,
>   plotting to kill me.

14 But my trust is in you, O LORD;
>   you are my God.
15 I am always in your care;
>   save me from my enemies,
>   from those who persecute me.
16 Look on your servant with kindness;
>   save me in your constant love.
17 I call to you, LORD;
>   don't let me be disgraced.

w Some ancient translations troubles; Hebrew iniquity.

May the wicked be disgraced;
　　may they go silently down to the world of
　　　the dead.
18 Silence those liars—
　　all the proud and arrogant
　　who speak with contempt about the
　　　righteous.

19 How wonderful are the good things
　　you keep for those who honor you!
Everyone knows how good you are,
　　how securely you protect those who
　　　trust you.
20 You hide them in the safety of your presence
　　from the plots of others;
in a safe shelter you hide them
　　from the insults of their enemies.

21 Praise the LORD!
How wonderfully he showed his love for me
　　when I was surrounded and attacked!
22 I was afraid and thought
　　that he had driven me out of his presence.
But he heard my cry,
　　when I called to him for help.

23 Love the LORD, all his faithful people.
The LORD protects the faithful,
　　but punishes the proud as they deserve.
24 Be strong, be courageous,
　　all you that hope in the LORD.

Confession and Forgiveness [x]

32 Happy are those whose sins are forgiven,
 whose wrongs are pardoned.
2 Happy is the one whom the LORD does not
 accuse of doing wrong
 and who is free from all deceit.

3 When I did not confess my sins,
 I was worn out from crying all day long.
4 Day and night you punished me, LORD;
 my strength was completely drained,
 as moisture is dried up by the summer heat.

5 Then I confessed my sins to you;
 I did not conceal my wrongdoings.
 I decided to confess them to you,
 and you forgave all my sins.

6 So all your loyal people should pray to you in
 times of need; [y]
 when a great flood of trouble comes
 rushing in,
 it will not reach them.
7 You are my hiding place;
 you will save me from trouble.
 I sing aloud of your salvation,
 because you protect me.

8 The LORD says, "I will teach you the way you
 should go;
 I will instruct you and advise you.

---

[x] HEBREW TITLE: *A poem by David.*   [y] *Some ancient translations* need; *Hebrew* finding
only.

⁹ Don't be stupid like a horse or a mule,
    which must be controlled with a bit and
        bridle
    to make it submit."

¹⁰ The wicked will have to suffer,
    but those who trust in the LORD
    are protected by his constant love.
¹¹ You that are righteous, be glad and rejoice
    because of what the LORD has done.
    You that obey him, shout for joy!

A Song of Praise

33 All you that are righteous,
        shout for joy for what the LORD has
            done;
    praise him, all you that obey him.
² Give thanks to the LORD with harps,
    sing to him with stringed instruments.
³ Sing a new song to him,
    play the harp with skill, and shout for joy!

⁴ The words of the LORD are true,
    and all his works are dependable.
⁵ The LORD loves what is righteous and just;
    his constant love fills the earth.

⁶ The LORD created the heavens by his
        command,
    the sun, moon, and stars by his spoken
        word.
⁷ He gathered all the seas into one place;

he shut up the ocean depths in storerooms.

8 Worship the LORD, all the earth!
   Honor him, all peoples of the world!
9 When he spoke, the world was created;
   at his command everything appeared.

10 The LORD frustrates the purposes of the
        nations;
     he keeps them from carrying out their
        plans.
11 But his plans endure forever;
     his purposes last eternally.
12 Happy is the nation whose God is the LORD;
     happy are the people he has chosen for
        his own!

13 The LORD looks down from heaven
     and sees all of us humans.
14 From where he rules, he looks down
     on all who live on earth.
15 He forms all their thoughts
     and knows everything they do.

16 A king does not win because of his powerful
        army;
     a soldier does not triumph because of his
        strength.
17 War horses are useless for victory;
     their great strength cannot save.

18 The LORD watches over those who obey him,
     those who trust in his constant love.

19 He saves them from death;
 he keeps them alive in times of famine.

20 We put our hope in the LORD;
 he is our protector and our help.
21 We are glad because of him;
 we trust in his holy name.

22 May your constant love be with us, LORD,
 as we put our hope in you.

In Praise of God's Goodness [z]

34 I will always thank the LORD;
  I will never stop praising him.
2 I will praise him for what he has done;
 may all who are oppressed listen and be
  glad!
3 Proclaim with me the LORD's greatness;
 let us praise his name together!

4 I prayed to the LORD, and he answered me;
 he freed me from all my fears.
5 The oppressed look to him and are glad;
 they will never be disappointed.
6 The helpless call to him, and he answers;
 he saves them from all their troubles.
7 His angel guards those who honor the LORD
 and rescues them from danger.

8 Find out for yourself how good the LORD is.
 Happy are those who find safety with him.

[z] HEBREW TITLE: *By David, who left the presence of Abimelech after pretending to be crazy and being sent away by him.*

9 Honor the LORD, all his people;
  those who obey him have all they need.
10 Even lions go hungry for lack of food,
  but those who obey the LORD lack nothing
    good.

11 Come, my young friends, and listen to me,
  and I will teach you to honor the LORD.
12 Would you like to enjoy life?
  Do you want long life and happiness?
13 Then keep from speaking evil
  and from telling lies.
14 Turn away from evil and do good;
  strive for peace with all your heart.

15 The LORD watches over the righteous
  and listens to their cries;
16 but he opposes those who do evil,
  so that when they die, they are soon
    forgotten.
17 The righteous call to the LORD, and he listens;
  he rescues them from all their troubles.
18 The LORD is near to those who are
    discouraged;
  he saves those who have lost all hope.

19 Good people suffer many troubles,
  but the LORD saves them from them all;
20 the LORD preserves them completely;
  not one of their bones is broken.
21 Evil will kill the wicked;
  those who hate the righteous will be
    punished.

22 The Lord will save his people;
    those who go to him for protection will be
        spared.

A Prayer for Help [a]

35 Oppose those who oppose me, Lord,
        and fight those who fight against me!
2 Take your shield and armor
    and come to my rescue.
3 Lift up your spear and war ax
    against those who pursue me.
Promise that you will save me.

4 May those who try to kill me
    be defeated and disgraced!
May those who plot against me
    be turned back and confused!
5 May they be like straw blown by the wind
    as the angel of the Lord pursues them!
6 May their path be dark and slippery
    while the angel of the Lord strikes them
        down!

7 Without any reason they laid a trap for me
    and dug a deep hole to catch me.
8 But destruction will catch them before they
        know it;
    they will be caught in their own trap
    and fall to their destruction!

9 Then I will be glad because of the Lord;

[a] HEBREW TITLE: *By David.*

I will be happy because he saved me.
10 With all my heart I will say to the LORD,
"There is no one like you.
You protect the weak from the strong,
the poor from the oppressor."

11 Evil people testify against me
and accuse me of crimes I know nothing
about.
12 They pay me back evil for good,
and I sink in despair.
13 But when they were sick, I dressed in
mourning;
I deprived myself of food;
I prayed with my head bowed low,
14   as I would pray for a friend or a brother.
I went around bent over in mourning,
as one who mourns for his mother.

15 But when I was in trouble, they were all glad
and gathered around to make fun of me;
strangers beat me
and kept striking me.
16 Like those who would mock a cripple, *b*
they glared at me with hate.

17 How much longer, Lord, will you just
look on?
Rescue me from their attacks;
save my life from these lions!

b Probable text Like those . . . cripple; *Hebrew unclear.*

18 Then I will thank you in the assembly of your
people;
I will praise you before them all.

19 Don't let my enemies, those liars,
gloat over my defeat.
Don't let those who hate me for no reason
smirk with delight over my sorrow.

20 They do not speak in a friendly way;
instead they invent all kinds of lies about
peace-loving people.
21 They accuse me, shouting,
"We saw what you did!"
22 But you, O LORD, have seen this.
So don't be silent, Lord;
don't keep yourself far away!
23 Rouse yourself, O Lord, and defend me;
rise up, my God, and plead my cause.
24 You are righteous, O LORD, so declare me
innocent;
don't let my enemies gloat over me.
25 Don't let them say to themselves,
"We are rid of him!
That's just what we wanted!"

26 May those who gloat over my suffering
be completely defeated and confused;
may those who claim to be better than I am
be covered with shame and disgrace.

27 May those who want to see me acquitted
shout for joy and say again and again,

"How great is the LORD!
    He is pleased with the success of his
        servant."
28 Then I will proclaim your righteousness,
    and I will praise you all day long.

Human Wickedness [c]

36 Sin speaks to the wicked deep in their
            hearts;
    they reject God and do not have reverence
        for him.
2 Because they think so highly of themselves,
    they think that God will not discover their
        sin and condemn it.
3 Their speech is wicked and full of lies;
    they no longer do what is wise and good.
4 They make evil plans as they lie in bed;
    nothing they do is good,
    and they never reject anything evil.

The Goodness of God

5 LORD, your constant love reaches the
            heavens;
    your faithfulness extends to the skies.
6 Your righteousness is towering like the
            mountains;
    your justice is like the depths of the sea.
    People and animals are in your care.

7 How precious, O God, is your constant love!

c HEBREW TITLE: *By David, the LORD's servant.*

We find[d] protection under the shadow of
    your wings.
8 We feast on the abundant food you provide;
    you let us drink from the river of your
      goodness.
9 You are the source of all life,
    and because of your light we see the light.

10 Continue to love those who know you
    and to do good to those who are righteous.
11 Do not let proud people attack me
    or the wicked make me run away.

12 See where evil people have fallen.
    There they lie, unable to rise.

The Destiny of the Wicked and of the Good[e]

37 Don't be worried on account of the
        wicked;
    don't be jealous of those who do wrong.
2 They will soon disappear like grass that
      dries up;
    they will die like plants that wither.

3 Trust in the LORD and do good;
    live in the land and be safe.
4 Seek your happiness in the LORD,
    and he will give you your heart's desire.

5 Give yourself to the LORD;
    trust in him, and he will help you;

[d] precious, O God, is . . . find; *or* precious is your constant love! Gods and people find.
[e] HEBREW TITLE: *By David.*

6 he will make your righteousness shine like the
    noonday sun.

7 Be patient and wait for the LORD to act;
    don't be worried about those who prosper
    or those who succeed in their evil plans.

8 Don't give in to worry or anger;
    it only leads to trouble.
9 Those who trust in the LORD will possess the
    land,
    but the wicked will be driven out.

10 Soon the wicked will disappear;
    you may look for them, but you won't find
    them;
11 but the humble will possess the land
    and enjoy prosperity and peace.

12 The wicked plot against good people
    and glare at them with hate.
13 But the Lord laughs at wicked people,
    because he knows they will soon be
    destroyed.

14 The wicked draw their swords and bend their
    bows
    to kill the poor and needy,
    to slaughter those who do what is right;
15 but they will be killed by their own swords,
    and their bows will be smashed.

16 The little that a good person owns

is worth more than the wealth of all the
    wicked,
17 because the LORD will take away the strength
    of the wicked,
    but protect those who are good.

18 The LORD takes care of those who obey him,
    and the land will be theirs forever.
19 They will not suffer when times are bad;
    they will have enough in time of famine.
20 But the wicked will die;
    the enemies of the LORD will vanish like
    wild flowers;
    they will disappear like smoke.

21 The wicked borrow and never pay back,
    but good people are generous with their
    gifts.
22 Those who are blessed by the LORD will
    possess the land,
    but those who are cursed by him will be
    driven out.

23 The LORD guides us in the way we should go
    and protects those who please him.
24 If they fall, they will not stay down,
    because the LORD will help them up.

25 I am old now; I have lived a long time,
    but I have never seen good people
    abandoned by the LORD
    or their children begging for food.

26 At all times they give freely and lend to
        others,
      and their children are a blessing.

27 Turn away from evil and do good,
      and your descendants will always live in the
        land;
28 for the LORD loves what is right
      and does not abandon his faithful people.
    He protects them forever,
      but the descendants of the wicked will be
        driven out.
29 The righteous will possess the land
      and live in it forever.

30 The words of good people are wise,
      and they are always fair.
31 They keep the law of their God in their hearts
      and never depart from it.

32 Wicked people watch good people
      and try to kill them;
33 but the LORD will not abandon them to their
        enemy's power
      or let them be condemned when they are
        on trial.

34 Put your hope in the LORD and obey his
        commands;
      he will honor you by giving you the land,
      and you will see the wicked driven out.

35 I once knew someone wicked who was a
    tyrant;
    he towered over everyone like a cedar of
    Lebanon;*f*
36 but later I*g* passed by, and he wasn't there;
    I looked for him, but couldn't find him.

37 Notice good people, observe the righteous;
    peaceful people have descendants,
38 but sinners are completely destroyed,
    and their descendants are wiped out.

39 The LORD saves the righteous
    and protects them in times of trouble.
40 He helps them and rescues them;
    he saves them from the wicked,
    because they go to him for protection.

The Prayer of a Sufferer *h*

38 O LORD, don't punish me in your anger!
  2 You have wounded me with your arrows;
    you have struck me down.

3 Because of your anger, I am in great pain;
    my whole body is diseased because of my
    sins.
4 I am drowning in the flood of my sins;
    they are a burden too heavy to bear.

5 Because I have been foolish,

---

f One ancient translation like a cedar of Lebanon; *Hebrew unclear.*
g Some ancient translations I; *Hebrew* he.   *h* HEBREW TITLE: *A psalm by David;*
a lament.

　　　my sores stink and rot.
6 I am bent over, I am crushed;
　　　I mourn all day long.
7 I am burning with fever
　　　and I am near death.
8 I am worn out and utterly crushed;
　　　my heart is troubled, and I groan with pain.

9 O Lord, you know what I long for;
　　　you hear all my groans.
10 My heart is pounding, my strength is gone,
　　　and my eyes have lost their brightness.
11 My friends and neighbors will not come
　　　　　near me,
　　　because of my sores;
　　　even my family keeps away from me.
12 Those who want to kill me lay traps for me,
　　　and those who want to hurt me threaten to
　　　　　ruin me;
　　　they never stop plotting against me.

13 I am like the deaf and cannot hear,
　　　like the dumb and cannot speak.
14 I am like those who do not answer,
　　　because they cannot hear.

15 But I trust in you, O LORD;
　　　and you, O Lord my God, will answer me.
16 Don't let my enemies gloat over my distress;
　　　don't let them boast about my downfall!

¹⁷ I am about to fall
    and am in constant pain.

¹⁸ I confess my sins;
    they fill me with anxiety.
¹⁹ My enemies are healthy and strong;
    there are many who hate me for no reason.
²⁰ Those who pay back evil for good
    are against me because I try to do right.

²¹ Do not abandon me, O LORD;
    do not stay away, my God!
²² Help me now, O Lord my savior!

The Confession of a Sufferer[i]

39 I said, "I will be careful about what I do
    and will not let my tongue make me sin;
I will not say anything
    while evil people are near."
² I kept quiet, not saying a word,
    not even about anything good!
But my suffering only grew worse,
³   and I was overcome with anxiety.
The more I thought, the more troubled I
      became;
    I could not keep from asking:
⁴ "LORD, how long will I live?
    When will I die?
    Tell me how soon my life will end."

---

[i] HEBREW TITLE: *A psalm by David.*

⁵ How short you have made my life!
    In your sight my lifetime seems nothing.
    Indeed every living being is no more than a
        puff of wind,
⁶   no more than a shadow.
    All we do is for nothing;
        we gather wealth, but don't know who will
        get it.

⁷ What, then, can I hope for, Lord?
    I put my hope in you.
⁸ Save me from all my sins,
    and don't let fools make fun of me.
⁹ I will keep quiet, I will not say a word,
    for you are the one who made me suffer
        like this.
¹⁰ Don't punish me any more!
    I am about to die from your blows.
¹¹ You punish our sins by your rebukes,
    and like a moth you destroy what we love.
    Indeed we are no more than a puff of wind!

¹² Hear my prayer, LORD,
    and listen to my cry;
    come to my aid when I weep.
    Like all my ancestors
        I am only your guest for a little while.
¹³ Leave me alone so that I may have some
        happiness
    before I go away and am no more.

A Song of Praise [i]

40 I waited patiently for the LORD's help;
  then he listened to me and heard
   my cry.
2 He pulled me out of a dangerous pit,
  out of the deadly quicksand.
He set me safely on a rock
  and made me secure.
3 He taught me to sing a new song,
  a song of praise to our God.
Many who see this will take warning
  and will put their trust in the LORD.

4 Happy are those who trust the LORD,
  who do not turn to idols
  or join those who worship false gods.
5 You have done many things for us, O LORD
  our God;
  there is no one like you!
  You have made many wonderful plans
   for us.
I could never speak of them all—
  their number is so great!

6 You do not want sacrifices and offerings;
  you do not ask for animals burned whole
   on the altar
  or for sacrifices to take away sins.
Instead, you have given me ears to hear you,
7 and so I answered, "Here I am;

---

i HEBREW TITLE: *A psalm by David.*

your instructions for me are in the book of
the Law.*j*
8 How I love to do your will, my God!
I keep your teaching in my heart."

9 In the assembly of all your people, LORD,
I told the good news that you save us.
You know that I will never stop telling it.
10 I have not kept the news of salvation to
myself;
I have always spoken of your faithfulness
and help.
In the assembly of all your people I have not
been silent
about your loyalty and constant love.

11 LORD, I know you will never stop being
merciful to me.
Your love and loyalty will always keep me
safe.

A Prayer for Help
(Psalm 70)

12 I am surrounded by many troubles—
too many to count!
My sins have caught up with me,
and I can no longer see;
they are more than the hairs of my head,
and I have lost my courage.
13 Save me, LORD! Help me now!
14 May those who try to kill me

j your instructions . . . Law; *or* my devotion to you is recorded in your book.

be completely defeated and confused.
May those who are happy because of my
    troubles
be turned back and disgraced.
15 May those who make fun of me
    be dismayed by their defeat.

16 May all who come to you
    be glad and joyful.
May all who are thankful for your salvation
    always say, "How great is the LORD!"

17 I am weak and poor, O Lord,
    but you have not forgotten me.
You are my savior and my God—
    hurry to my aid!

A Prayer in Sickness [k]

41 Happy are those who are concerned for
    the poor;
    the LORD will help them when they are in
    trouble.
2 The LORD will protect them and preserve their
    lives;
    he will make them happy in the land;
    he will not abandon them to the power of
    their enemies.
3 The LORD will help them when they are sick
    and will restore them to health.

[k] HEBREW TITLE: *A psalm by David.*

⁴ I said, "I have sinned against you, Lord;
    be merciful to me and heal me."
⁵ My enemies say cruel things about me.
    They want me to die and be forgotten.
⁶ Those who come to see me are not sincere;
    they gather bad news about me
    and then go out and tell it everywhere.
⁷ All who hate me whisper to each other
      about me,
    they imagine the worst about*l* me.
⁸ They say, "He is fatally ill;
    he will never leave his bed again."
⁹ Even my best friend, the one I trusted most,
    the one who shared my food,
    has turned against me.

¹⁰ Be merciful to me, Lord, and restore my
      health,
    and I will pay my enemies back.
¹¹ They will not triumph over me,
    and I will know that you are pleased
      with me.
¹² You will help me, because I do what is right;
    you will keep me in your presence forever.

¹³ Praise the Lord, the God of Israel!
    Praise him now and forever!

Amen! Amen!

---

l imagine the worst about; *or* make evil plans to harm.

BOOK TWO
(Psalms 42–72)

The Prayer of Someone in Exile [m]

42 As a deer longs for a stream of cool
water,
so I long for you, O God.
2 I thirst for you, the living God.
When can I go and worship in your
presence?
3 Day and night I cry,
and tears are my only food;
all the time my enemies ask me,
"Where is your God?"

4 My heart breaks when I remember the past,
when I went with the crowds to the house
of God
and led them as they walked along,
a happy crowd, singing and shouting praise
to God.
5 Why am I so sad?
Why am I so troubled?
I will put my hope in God,
and once again I will praise him,
my savior and my God.

6-7 Here in exile my heart is breaking,
and so I turn my thoughts to him.
He has sent waves of sorrow over my soul;
chaos roars at me like a flood,

[m] HEBREW TITLE: *A poem by the clan of Korah.*

like waterfalls thundering down to the
    Jordan
from Mount Hermon and Mount Mizar.
8 May the LORD show his constant love during
      the day,
  so that I may have a song at night,
  a prayer to the God of my life.

9 To God, my defender, I say,
  "Why have you forgotten me?
Why must I go on suffering
  from the cruelty of my enemies?"
10 I am crushed by their insults,
  as they keep on asking me,
  "Where is your God?"

11 Why am I so sad?
  Why am I so troubled?
I will put my hope in God,
  and once again I will praise him,
  my savior and my God.

The Prayer of Someone in Exile
(Continuation of Psalm 42)

43 O God, declare me innocent,
    and defend my cause against the
      ungodly;
  deliver me from lying and evil people!
2 You are my protector;
  why have you abandoned me?
Why must I go on suffering
  from the cruelty of my enemies?

3 Send your light and your truth;
    may they lead me
    and bring me back to Zion, your sacred
        hill,[n]
    and to your Temple, where you live.
4 Then I will go to your altar, O God;
    you are the source of my happiness.
I will play my harp and sing praise to you,
    O God, my God.

5 Why am I so sad?
    Why am I so troubled?
I will put my hope in God,
    and once again I will praise him,
    my savior and my God.

A Prayer for Protection [o]

44 With our own ears we have heard it,
        O God—
    our ancestors have told us about it,
    about the great things you did in their time,
        in the days of long ago:
2 how you yourself drove out the heathen
        and established your people in their land;
    how you punished the other nations
        and caused your own to prosper.
3 Your people did not conquer the land with
        their swords;
    they did not win it by their own power;

[n] SACRED HILL: See 2.6.   [o] HEBREW TITLE: A poem by the clan of Korah.

it was by your power and your strength,
　　by the assurance of your presence,
　　which showed that you loved them.

4 You are my king and my God;
　　you give *p* victory to your people,
5 　　and by your power we defeat our enemies.
6 I do not trust in my bow
　　or in my sword to save me;
7 but you have saved us from our enemies
　　and defeated those who hate us.
8 We will always praise you
　　and give thanks to you forever.

9 But now you have rejected us and let us be
　　　defeated;
　　you no longer march out with our armies.
10 You made us run from our enemies,
　　and they took for themselves what was
　　　ours.
11 You allowed us to be slaughtered like sheep;
　　you scattered us in foreign countries.
12 You sold your own people for a small price
　　as though they had little value. *q*

13 Our neighbors see what you did to us,
　　and they mock us and laugh at us.
14 You have made us a joke among the nations;
　　they shake their heads at us in scorn.

p Some ancient translations and my God; you give; *Hebrew* O God; give.
q as . . . value; or and made no profit from the sale.

15 I am always in disgrace;
    I am covered with shame
16   from hearing the sneers and insults
    of my enemies and those who hate me.

17 All this has happened to us,
    even though we have not forgotten you
    or broken the covenant you made with us.
18 We have not been disloyal to you;
    we have not disobeyed your commands.
19 Yet you left us helpless among wild animals;
    you abandoned us in deepest darkness.

20 If we had stopped worshiping our God
    and prayed to a foreign god,
21 you would surely have discovered it,
    because you know our secret thoughts.
22 But it is on your account that we are being
    killed all the time,
    that we are treated like sheep to be
    slaughtered.

23 Wake up, Lord! Why are you asleep?
    Rouse yourself! Don't reject us forever!
24 Why are you hiding from us?
    Don't forget our suffering and trouble!

25 We fall crushed to the ground;
    we lie defeated in the dust.
26 Come to our aid!
    Because of your constant love save us!

A Royal Wedding Song [r]

45 Beautiful words fill my mind,
  as I compose this song for the king.
 Like the pen of a good writer
  my tongue is ready with a poem.

2 You are the most handsome of men;
  you are an eloquent speaker.
  God has always blessed you.
3 Buckle on your sword, mighty king;
  you are glorious and majestic.

4 Ride on in majesty to victory
  for the defense of truth and justice! [s]
  Your strength will win you great victories!
5 Your arrows are sharp,
  they pierce the hearts of your enemies;
  nations fall down at your feet.

6 The kingdom that God has given you [t]
  will last forever and ever.
 You rule over your people with justice;
7 you love what is right and hate what is evil.
 That is why God, your God, has chosen you
  and has poured out more happiness on you
  than on any other king.
8 The perfume of myrrh and aloes is on your
  clothes;

---

[r] HEBREW TITLE: *A poem by the clan of Korah; a love song.* [s] *Probable text* and justice; *Hebrew* and meekness of justice. [t] The kingdom that God has given you; *or* Your kingdom, O God; *or* Your divine kingdom.

musicians entertain you in palaces
decorated with ivory.
9 Among the women of your court are
daughters of kings,
and at the right of your throne stands the
queen,
wearing ornaments of finest gold.

10 Bride of the king, listen to what I say—
forget your people and your relatives.
11 Your beauty will make the king desire you;
he is your master, so you must obey him.
12 The people of Tyre will bring you gifts;
rich people will try to win your favor.

13 The princess is in the palace—how beautiful
she is!
Her gown is made of gold thread.
14 In her colorful gown she is led to the king,
followed by her bridesmaids,
and they also are brought to him.
15 With joy and gladness they come
and enter the king's palace.

16 You, my king, will have many sons
to succeed your ancestors as kings,
and you will make them rulers over the
whole earth.
17 My song will keep your fame alive forever,
and everyone will praise you for all time to
come.

God Is with Us [u]

46 God is our shelter and strength,
　　　always ready to help in times of trouble.
2 So we will not be afraid, even if the earth is
　　　shaken
　　and mountains fall into the ocean depths;
3 even if the seas roar and rage,
　　and the hills are shaken by the violence.

4 There is a river that brings joy to the city
　　　of God,
　　to the sacred house of the Most High.
5 God is in that city, and it will never be
　　　destroyed;
　　at early dawn he will come to its aid.
6 Nations are terrified, kingdoms are shaken;
　　God thunders, and the earth dissolves.

7 The LORD Almighty is with us;
　　the God of Jacob is our refuge.

8 Come and see what the LORD has done.
　　See what amazing things he has done on
　　　earth.
9 He stops wars all over the world;
　　he breaks bows, destroys spears,
　　and sets shields on fire.
10 "Stop fighting," he says, "and know that I
　　　am God,
　　supreme among the nations,
　　supreme over the world."

[u] HEBREW TITLE: *A song by the clan of Korah.*

11 The LORD Almighty is with us;
    the God of Jacob is our refuge.

The Supreme Ruler [v]

47 Clap your hands for joy, all peoples!
        Praise God with loud songs!
2 The LORD, the Most High, is to be feared;
    he is a great king, ruling over all the world.
3 He gave us victory over the peoples;
    he made us rule over the nations.
4 He chose for us the land where we live,
    the proud possession of his people, whom
        he loves.

5 God goes up to his throne.
    There are shouts of joy and the blast of
        trumpets,
    as the LORD goes up.
6 Sing praise to God;
    sing praise to our king!
7 God is king over all the world;
    praise him with songs!

8 God sits on his sacred throne;
    he rules over the nations.
9 The rulers of the nations assemble
    with the people [w] of the God of Abraham.
    More powerful than all armies is he;
        he rules supreme.

[v] HEBREW TITLE: *A psalm by the clan of Korah.*   [w] *Probable text* with the people;
Hebrew the people.

Zion, the City of God [x]

48 The LORD is great and is to be highly
praised
in the city of our God, on his sacred hill. [y]
2 Zion, the mountain of God, is high and
beautiful;
the city of the great king brings joy to all
the world.
3 God has shown that there is safety with him
inside the fortresses of the city.

4 The kings gathered together
and came to attack Mount Zion.
5 But when they saw it, they were amazed;
they were afraid and ran away.
6 There they were seized with fear and anguish,
like a woman about to bear a child,
7   like ships tossing in a furious storm.

8 We have heard what God has done,
and now we have seen it
in the city of our God, the LORD Almighty;
he will keep the city safe forever.

9 Inside your Temple, O God,
we think of your constant love.
10 You are praised by people everywhere,
and your fame extends over all the earth.
You rule with justice;
11   let the people of Zion be glad!

[x] HEBREW TITLE: *A psalm by the clan of Korah; a song.*   [y] SACRED HILL: *See 2.6.*

You give right judgments;
   let there be joy in the cities of Judah!

12 People of God, walk around Zion and count
     the towers;
13   take notice of the walls and examine the
     fortresses,
so that you may tell the next generation:
14   "This God is our God forever and ever;
   he will lead us for all time to come."

The Foolishness of Trusting in Riches z

49 Hear this, everyone!
   Listen, all people everywhere,
2   great and small alike,
   rich and poor together.
3 My thoughts will be clear;
   I will speak words of wisdom.
4 I will turn my attention to proverbs
   and explain their meaning as I play the
     harp.

5 I am not afraid in times of danger
   when I am surrounded by enemies,
6 by evil people who trust in their riches
   and boast of their great wealth.
7 We can never redeem ourselves;
   we cannot pay God the price for our lives,
8   because the payment for a human life is too
     great.
What we could pay would never be enough

z HEBREW TITLE: *A psalm by the clan of Korah.*

9   to keep us from the grave,
     to let us live forever.

10 Anyone can see that even the wise die,
     as well as the foolish and stupid.
     They all leave their riches to their
          descendants.
11 Their graves *a* are their homes forever;
     there they stay for all time,
     though they once had lands of their own.
12 Our greatness cannot keep us from death;
     we will still die like the animals.

13 See what happens to those who trust in
          themselves,
     the fate of those *b* who are satisfied with
          their wealth—
14 they are doomed to die like sheep,
     and Death will be their shepherd.
   The righteous will triumph over them,
     as their bodies quickly decay
     in the world of the dead far from their
          homes. *c*
15 But God will rescue me;
     he will save me from the power of death.

16 Don't be upset when someone becomes rich,
     when his wealth grows even greater;
17 he cannot take it with him when he dies;
     his wealth will not go with him to the
          grave.
18 Even if someone is satisfied with this life

a Some ancient translations graves; *Hebrew* inner thoughts.   *b One ancient translation*
the fate of those; *Hebrew* after them.   *c* in . . . homes.; *Hebrew unclear.*

and is praised because he is successful,
19 he will join all his ancestors in death,
   where the darkness lasts forever.
20 Our greatness cannot keep us from death;
   we will still die like the animals.

True Worship ^d

50 The Almighty God, the LORD, speaks;
   he calls to the whole earth from east to
      west.
2 God shines from Zion,
   the city perfect in its beauty.

3 Our God is coming, but not in silence;
   a raging fire is in front of him,
   a furious storm around him.
4 He calls heaven and earth as witnesses
   to see him judge his people.
5 He says, "Gather my faithful people to me,
   those who made a covenant with me by
      offering a sacrifice."
6 The heavens proclaim that God is righteous,
   that he himself is judge.

7 "Listen, my people, and I will speak;
   I will testify against you, Israel.
   I am God, your God.
8 I do not reprimand you because of your
      sacrifices
   and the burnt offerings you always
      bring me.

d HEBREW TITLE: *A psalm by Asaph.*

9 And yet I do not need bulls from your farms
    or goats from your flocks;
10 all the animals in the forest are mine
    and the cattle on thousands of hills.
11 All the wild birds are mine
    and all living things in the fields.

12 "If I were hungry, I would not ask you for
    food,
    for the world and everything in it is mine.
13 Do I eat the flesh of bulls
    or drink the blood of goats?
14 Let the giving of thanks be your sacrifice
    to God,*e*
    and give the Almighty all that you
    promised.
15 Call to me when trouble comes;
    I will save you,
    and you will praise me."

16 But God says to the wicked,
    "Why should you recite my
    commandments?
    Why should you talk about my covenant?
17 You refuse to let me correct you;
    you reject my commands.
18 You become the friend of every thief you see,
    and you associate with adulterers.

19 "You are always ready to speak evil;
    you never hesitate to tell lies.

e Let the giving . . . to God; *or* Offer your thanksgiving sacrifice to God.

20 You are ready to accuse your own relatives
and to find fault with them.
21 You have done all this, and I have said
nothing,
so you thought that I am like you.
But now I reprimand you
and make the matter plain to you.

22 "Listen to this, you that ignore me,
or I will destroy you,
and there will be no one to save you.
23 Giving thanks is the sacrifice that honors me,
and I will surely save all who obey me."

A Prayer for Forgiveness*f*

51   Be merciful to me, O God,
    because of your constant love.
Because of your great mercy
wipe away my sins!
2 Wash away all my evil
and make me clean from my sin!

3 I recognize my faults;
I am always conscious of my sins.
4 I have sinned against you—only
against you—
and done what you consider evil.
So you are right in judging me;
you are justified in condemning me.
5 I have been evil from the day I was born;

f HEBREW TITLE: *A psalm by David, after the prophet Nathan had spoken to him about his adultery with Bathsheba.*

from the time I was conceived, I have been
  sinful.

⁶ Sincerity and truth are what you require;
  fill my mind with your wisdom.
⁷ Remove my sin, and I will be clean;
  wash me, and I will be whiter than snow.
⁸ Let me hear the sounds of joy and gladness;
  and though you have crushed me and
    broken me,
  I will be happy once again.
⁹ Close your eyes to my sins
  and wipe out all my evil.

¹⁰ Create a pure heart in me, O God,
  and put a new and loyal spirit in me.
¹¹ Do not banish me from your presence;
  do not take your holy spirit away from me.
¹² Give me again the joy that comes from your
    salvation,
  and make me willing to obey you.
¹³ Then I will teach sinners your commands,
  and they will turn back to you.

¹⁴ Spare my life, O God, and save me,ᵍ
  and I will gladly proclaim your
    righteousness.
¹⁵ Help me to speak, Lord,
  and I will praise you.

¹⁶ You do not want sacrifices,

ᵍ Spare my life . . . me; *or* O God my savior, keep me from the crime of murder.

or I would offer them;
   you are not pleased with burnt offerings.
17 My sacrifice is a humble spirit, O God;
      you will not reject a humble and repentant
         heart.

18 O God, be kind to Zion and help her;
      rebuild the walls of Jerusalem.
19 Then you will be pleased with proper
         sacrifices
      and with our burnt offerings;
      and bulls will be sacrificed on your altar.

God's Judgment and Grace [h]

52 Why do you boast, great one, of your
         evil?
   God's faithfulness is eternal.
2 You make plans to ruin others;
      your tongue is like a sharp razor.
      You are always inventing lies.
3 You love evil more than good
      and falsehood more than truth.
4 You love to hurt people with your words, you
         liar!

5 So God will ruin you forever;
      he will take hold of you and snatch you
         from your home;
      he will remove you from the world of the
         living.
6 Righteous people will see this and be afraid;

h HEBREW TITLE: *A poem by David, after Doeg the Edomite went to Saul and told him
that David had gone to the house of Ahimelech.*

then they will laugh at you and say,
⁷ "Look, here is someone who did not depend
      on God for safety,
   but trusted instead in great wealth
   and looked for security in being wicked."

⁸ But I am like an olive tree growing in the
      house of God;
   I trust in his constant love forever and
      ever.
⁹ I will always thank you, God, for what you
      have done;
   in the presence of your people
   I will proclaim that you are good.

Human Wickedness *i*
(Psalm 14)

53 Fools say to themselves,
         "There is no God."
   They are all corrupt,
      and they have done terrible things;
      there is no one who does what is right.

² God looks down from heaven at people
      to see if there are any who are wise,
      any who worship him.
³ But they have all turned away;
      they are all equally bad.
   Not one of them does what is right,
      not a single one.

i HEBREW TITLE: *A poem by David.*

4 "Don't they know?" God asks.
  "Are these evildoers ignorant?
They live by robbing my people,
  and they never pray to me."

5 But then they will become terrified,
   as they have never been before,
   for God will scatter the bones of the
     enemies of his people.
God has rejected them,
   and so Israel will totally defeat them.

6 How I pray that victory
   will come to Israel from Zion.
How happy the people of Israel will be
   when God makes them prosperous again!

A Prayer for Protection from Enemies *j*

54 Save me by your power, O God;
     set me free by your might!
2 Hear my prayer, O God;
   listen to my words!
3 Proud people are coming to attack me;
   cruel people are trying to kill me—
   those who do not care about God.

4 But God is my helper.
   The Lord is my defender.
5 May God use their own evil to punish my
     enemies.
   He will destroy them because he is faithful.

j HEBREW TITLE: *A poem by David, after the men from Ziph went to Saul and told him that David was hiding in their territory.*

⁶ I will gladly offer you a sacrifice, O LORD;
    I will give you thanks
    because you are good.
⁷ You have rescued me from all my troubles,
    and I have seen my enemies defeated.

The Prayer of Someone Betrayed by a Friend ᵏ

55 Hear my prayer, O God;
        don't turn away from my plea!
² Listen to me and answer me;
    I am worn out by my worries.
³ I am terrified by the threats of my enemies,
    crushed by the oppression of the wicked.
  They bring trouble on me;
    they are angry with me and hate me.

⁴ I am terrified,
    and the terrors of death crush me.
⁵ I am gripped by fear and trembling;
    I am overcome with horror.
⁶ I wish I had wings like a dove.
    I would fly away and find rest.
⁷ I would fly far away
    and make my home in the desert.
⁸ I would hurry and find myself a shelter
    from the raging wind and the storm.
⁹ Confuse the speech of my enemies, O Lord!

  I see violence and riots in the city,
¹⁰   surrounding it day and night,
    filling it with crime and trouble.

ᵏ HEBREW TITLE: *A poem by David.*

11 There is destruction everywhere;
    the streets are full of oppression and fraud.

12 If it were an enemy making fun of me,
    I could endure it;
  if it were an opponent boasting over me,
    I could hide myself from him.
13 But it is you, my companion,
    my colleague and close friend.
14 We had intimate talks with each other
    and worshiped together in the Temple.
15 May my enemies die before their time;
    may they go down alive into the world of
      the dead!
Evil is in their homes and in their hearts.

16 But I call to the LORD God for help,
    and he will save me.
17 Morning, noon, and night
    my complaints and groans go up to him,
    and he will hear my voice.
18 He will bring me safely back
    from the battles that I fight
    against so many enemies.
19 God, who has ruled from eternity,
    will hear me and defeat them;
  for they refuse to change,
    and they do not fear him.

20 My former companion attacked his friends;
    he broke his promises.
21 His words were smoother than cream,
    but there was hatred in his heart;

his words were as soothing as oil,
    but they cut like sharp swords.

22 Leave your troubles with the LORD,
    and he will defend you;
    he never lets honest people be defeated.

23 But you, O God, will bring those murderers
    and liars to their graves
    before half their life is over.
As for me, I will trust in you.

A Prayer of Trust in God [l]

56 Be merciful to me, O God,
    because I am under attack;
    my enemies persecute me all the time.
2 All day long my opponents attack me.
    There are so many who fight against me.
3 When I am afraid, O LORD Almighty,
    I put my trust in you.
4 I trust in God and am not afraid;
    I praise him for what he has promised.
    What can a mere human being do to me?

5 My enemies make trouble for me all day long;
    they are always thinking up some way to
       hurt me!
6 They gather in hiding places
    and watch everything I do,
    hoping to kill me.
7 Punish[m] them, O God, for their evil;

l HEBREW TITLE: *A psalm by David, after the Philistines captured him in Gath.*
m *Probable text* Punish; *Hebrew* Save.

defeat those people in your anger!

8 You know how troubled I am;
    you have kept a record of my tears.
    Aren't they listed in your book?
9 The day I call to you,
    my enemies will be turned back.
  I know this: God[n] is on my side—
10   the LORD, whose promises I praise.
11 In him I trust, and I will not be afraid.
    What can a mere human being do to me?

12 O God, I will offer you what I have promised;
    I will give you my offering of thanksgiving,
13 because you have rescued me from death
    and kept me from defeat.
  And so I walk in the presence of God,
    in the light that shines on the living.

A Prayer for Help[o]

57 Be merciful to me, O God, be merciful,
    because I come to you for safety.
In the shadow of your wings I find protection
    until the raging storms are over.

2 I call to God, the Most High,
    to God, who supplies my every need.
3 He will answer from heaven and save me;
    he will defeat my oppressors.
  God will show me his constant love and
    faithfulness.

---

[n] I know this: God; *or* Because I know that God.   [o] HEBREW TITLE: *A psalm by David, after he fled from Saul in the cave.*

⁴ I am surrounded by enemies,
 who are like lions hungry for human flesh.
Their teeth are like spears and arrows;
 their tongues are like sharp swords.

⁵ Show your greatness in the sky, O God,
 and your glory over all the earth.

⁶ My enemies have spread a net to catch me;
 I am overcome with distress.
They dug a pit in my path,
 but fell into it themselves.

⁷ I have complete confidence, O God;
 I will sing and praise you!
⁸ Wake up, my soul!
 Wake up, my harp and lyre!
 I will wake up the sun.
⁹ I will thank you, O Lord, among the nations.
 I will praise you among the peoples.
¹⁰ Your constant love reaches the heavens;
 your faithfulness touches the skies.
¹¹ Show your greatness in the sky, O God,
 and your glory over all the earth.

A Prayer for God to Punish the Wicked[p]

58 Do you rulers[q] ever give a just decision?
 Do you judge everyone fairly?
² No! You think only of the evil you can do,
 and commit crimes of violence in the land.

[p] HEBREW TITLE: *A psalm by David.*   [q] rulers; *or* gods.

3 Evildoers go wrong all their lives;
    they tell lies from the day they are born.
4 They are full of poison like snakes;
    they stop up their ears like a deaf cobra,
5 which does not hear the voice of the snake
        charmer,
    or the chant of the clever magician.

6 Break the teeth of these fierce lions, O God.
7 May they disappear like water draining away;
    may they be crushed like weeds on a
        path.*r*
8 May they be like snails that dissolve into
        slime;
    may they be like a baby born dead that
    never sees the light.
9 Before they know it, they are cut down like
        weeds;
    in his fierce anger God will blow them
    away
    while they are still living.*s*

10 The righteous will be glad when they see
        sinners punished;
    they will wade through the blood of the
        wicked.
11 People will say, "The righteous are indeed
        rewarded;
    there is indeed a God who judges the
        world."

r Probable text may . . . path; *Hebrew unclear.*   *s Verse 9 in Hebrew is unclear.*

A Prayer for Safety [t]

59 Save me from my enemies, my God;
     protect me from those who attack me!
2 Save me from those evil people;
     rescue me from those murderers!

3 Look! They are waiting to kill me;
     cruel people are gathering against me.
It is not because of any sin or wrong I have
       done,
4   nor because of any fault of mine, O LORD,
     that they hurry to their places.

5 Rise, LORD God Almighty, and come to
       my aid;
     see for yourself, God of Israel!
Wake up and punish the heathen;
     show no mercy to evil traitors!

6 They come back in the evening,
     snarling like dogs as they go about the city.
7 Listen to their insults and threats.
Their tongues are like swords in their mouths,
     yet they think that no one hears them.

8 But you laugh at them, LORD;
     you mock all the heathen.
9 I have confidence in your strength;
     you are my refuge, O God.

[t] HEBREW TITLE: *A psalm by David, after Saul sent men to watch his house in order to kill him.*

10 My God loves me and will come to me;
    he will let me see my enemies defeated.

11 Do not kill them, O God, or my people may
    forget.
    Scatter them by your strength and defeat
    them,
    O Lord, our protector.
12 Sin is on their lips; all their words are sinful;
    may they be caught in their pride!
    Because they curse and lie,
13   destroy them in your anger;
    destroy them completely.
    Then everyone will know that God rules in
    Israel,
    that his rule extends over all the earth.

14 My enemies come back in the evening,
    snarling like dogs as they go about the city,
15   like dogs roaming about for food
    and growling if they do not find enough.

16 But I will sing about your strength;
    every morning I will sing aloud of your
    constant love.
    You have been a refuge for me,
    a shelter in my time of trouble.
17 I will praise you, my defender.
    My refuge is God,
    the God who loves me.

A Prayer for Deliverance [u]

60 You have rejected us, God, and
defeated us;
you have been angry with us—but now
turn back to us. [v]

2 You have made the land tremble, and you
have cut it open;
now heal its wounds, because it is falling
apart.

3 You have made your people suffer greatly;
we stagger around as though we were
drunk.

4 You have warned those who have reverence
for you,
so that they might escape destruction.

5 Save us by your might; answer our prayer,
so that the people you love may be
rescued.

6 From his sanctuary [w] God has said,
"In triumph I will divide Shechem
and distribute Sukkoth Valley to my people.

7 Gilead is mine, and Manasseh too;
Ephraim is my helmet
and Judah my royal scepter.

8 But I will use Moab as my washbowl,
and I will throw my sandals on Edom,
as a sign that I own it.
Did the Philistines think they would shout in
triumph over me?"

[u] HEBREW TITLE: *A psalm by David, for teaching, when he fought against the Arameans from Naharaim and from Zobah, and Joab turned back and killed 12,000 Edomites in Salt Valley.* [v] angry with us . . . us; *or* angry with us and turned your back on us. [w] From his sanctuary; *or* In his holiness.

9 Who, O God, will take me into the fortified
       city?
   Who will lead me to Edom?
10 Have you really rejected us?
       Aren't you going to march out with our
           armies?
11 Help us against the enemy;
       human help is worthless.
12 With God on our side we will win;
       he will defeat our enemies.

A Prayer for Protection *x*

61 Hear my cry, O God;
           listen to my prayer!
2 In despair and far from home
       I call to you!

   Take me to a safe refuge,
3   for you are my protector,
       my strong defense against my enemies.

4 Let me live in your sanctuary all my life;
       let me find safety under your wings.
5 You have heard my promises, O God,
       and you have given me what belongs to
           those who honor you.

6 Add many years to the king's life;
       let him live on and on!

x HEBREW TITLE: *By David.*

7 May he rule forever in your presence, O God;
    protect him with your constant love and
       faithfulness.

8 So I will always sing praises to you,
    as I offer you daily what I have promised.

Confidence in God's Protection [y]

62   I wait patiently for God to save me;
        I depend on him alone.
2 He alone protects and saves me;
    he is my defender,
    and I shall never be defeated.

3 How much longer will all of you attack
      someone
    who is no stronger than a broken-down
      fence?
4 You only want to bring him down from his
      place of honor;
    you take pleasure in lies.
You speak words of blessing,
    but in your heart you curse him.

5 I depend on God alone;
    I put my hope in him.
6 He alone protects and saves me;
    he is my defender,
    and I shall never be defeated.
7 My salvation and honor depend on God;

y HEBREW TITLE: *A psalm by David.*

he is my strong protector;
he is my shelter.

8 Trust in God at all times, my people.
Tell him all your troubles,
for he is our refuge.

9 Human beings are all like a puff of breath;
great and small alike are worthless.
Put them on the scales, and they weigh
nothing;
they are lighter than a mere breath.
10 Don't put your trust in violence;
don't hope to gain anything by robbery;
even if your riches increase,
don't depend on them.

11 More than once I have heard God say
that power belongs to him
12   and that his love is constant.
You yourself, O Lord, reward everyone
according to their deeds.

Longing for God [z]

63 O God, you are my God,
and I long for you.
My whole being desires you;
like a dry, worn-out, and waterless land,
my soul is thirsty for you.
2 Let me see you in the sanctuary;

[z] HEBREW TITLE: *A psalm by David, when he was in the desert of Judea.*

let me see how mighty and glorious
    you are.
3 Your constant love is better than life itself,
    and so I will praise you.
4 I will give you thanks as long as I live;
    I will raise my hands to you in prayer.
5 My soul will feast and be satisfied,
    and I will sing glad songs of praise to you.

6 As I lie in bed, I remember you;
    all night long I think of you,
7   because you have always been my help.
In the shadow of your wings I sing for joy.
8 I cling to you,
    and your hand keeps me safe.

9 Those who are trying to kill me
    will go down into the world of the dead.
10 They will be killed in battle,
    and their bodies eaten by wolves.
11 Because God gives him victory,
    the king will rejoice.
Those who make promises in God's name will
    praise him,
    but the mouths of liars will be shut.

A Prayer for Protection [a]

64 I am in trouble, God—listen to my prayer!
    I am afraid of my enemies—save my
    life!
2 Protect me from the plots of the wicked,

[a] HEBREW TITLE: *A psalm by David.*

from mobs of evil people.

3 They sharpen their tongues like swords
and aim cruel words like arrows.
4 They are quick to spread their shameless
lies;
they destroy good people with cowardly
slander.
5 They encourage each other in their evil plots;
they talk about where they will place their
traps.
"No one can see them," they say.
6 They make evil plans and say,
"We have planned a perfect crime."
The human heart and mind are a mystery.

7 But God shoots his arrows at them,
and suddenly they are wounded.
8 He will destroy them because of those
words; b
all who see them will shake their heads.
9 They will all be afraid;
they will think about what God has done
and tell about his deeds.
10 All righteous people will rejoice
because of what the LORD has done.
They will find safety in him;
all good people will praise him.

b *Probable text* He will destroy them because of those words; *Hebrew* They will destroy
him, those words are against them.

Praise and Thanksgiving [c]

65 O God, it is right for us to praise you in
Zion
and keep our promises to you,
2   because you answer prayers.
People everywhere will come to you
3   on account of their sins.
Our faults defeat us,[d]
but you forgive them.
4 Happy are those whom you choose,
whom you bring to live in your sanctuary.
We shall be satisfied with the good things of
your house,
the blessings of your sacred Temple.

5 You answer us by giving us victory,
and you do wonderful things to save us.
People all over the world
and across the distant seas trust in you.
6 You set the mountains in place by your
strength,
showing your mighty power.
7 You calm the roar of the seas
and the noise of the waves;
you calm the uproar of the peoples.
8 The whole world stands in awe
of the great things that you have done.
Your deeds bring shouts of joy
from one end of the earth to the other.
9 You show your care for the land by sending
rain;

[c] HEBREW TITLE: *A psalm by David; a song.*   [d] *One ancient translation* us; *Hebrew* me.

you make it rich and fertile.
You fill the streams with water;
    you provide the earth with crops.
This is how you do it:
10   you send abundant rain on the plowed
       fields
    and soak them with water;
you soften the soil with showers
    and cause the young plants to grow.
11 What a rich harvest your goodness provides!
    Wherever you go there is plenty.
12 The pastures are filled with flocks;
    the hillsides are full of joy.
13 The fields are covered with sheep;
    the valleys are full of wheat.
Everything shouts and sings for joy.

A Song of Praise and Thanksgiving[e]

66 Praise God with shouts of joy, all people!
2 Sing to the glory of his name;
    offer him glorious praise!
3 Say to God, "How wonderful are the things
      you do!
    Your power is so great
    that your enemies bow down in fear
      before you.
4 Everyone on earth worships you;
    they sing praises to you,
    they sing praises to your name."

e HEBREW TITLE: *A song.*

⁵ Come and see what God has done,
  his wonderful acts among people.
⁶ He changed the sea into dry land;
  our ancestors crossed the river on foot.
There we rejoiced because of what he did.
⁷ He rules forever by his might
  and keeps his eyes on the nations.
Let no rebels rise against him.
⁸ Praise our God, all nations;
  let your praise be heard.
⁹ He has kept us alive
  and has not allowed us to fall.

¹⁰ You have put us to the test, God;
  as silver is purified by fire,
  so you have tested us.
¹¹ You let us fall into a trap
  and placed heavy burdens on our backs.
¹² You let our enemies trample us;
  we went through fire and flood,
  but now you have brought us to a place of
    safety.ᶠ

¹³ I will bring burnt offerings to your house;
  I will offer you what I promised.
¹⁴ I will give you what I said I would
  when I was in trouble.
¹⁵ I will offer sheep to be burned on the altar;
  I will sacrifice bulls and goats,
  and the smoke will go up to the sky.

ᶠ *Some ancient translations* safety; *Hebrew* overflowing.

16 Come and listen, all who honor God,
    and I will tell you what he has done for me.
17 I cried to him for help;
    I praised him with songs.
18 If I had ignored my sins,
    the Lord would not have listened to me.
19 But God has indeed heard me;
    he has listened to my prayer.

20 I praise God,
    because he did not reject my prayer
    or keep back his constant love from me.

A Song of Thanksgiving [g]

67 God, be merciful to us and bless us;
    look on us with kindness,
2 so that the whole world may know your will;
    so that all nations may know your
        salvation.

3 May the peoples praise you, O God;
    may all the peoples praise you!

4 May the nations be glad and sing for joy,
    because you judge the peoples with justice
    and guide every nation on earth.

5 May the peoples praise you, O God;
    may all the peoples praise you!

6 The land has produced its harvest;

[g] HEBREW TITLE: *A psalm; a song.*

God, our God, has blessed us.
7 God has blessed us;
    may all people everywhere honor him.

A National Song of Triumph *h*

68 God rises up and scatters his enemies.
        Those who hate him run away in defeat.
2 As smoke is blown away, so he drives
        them off;
    as wax melts in front of the fire,
    so do the wicked perish in God's presence.
3 But the righteous are glad and rejoice in his
        presence;
    they are happy and shout for joy.

4 Sing to God, sing praises to his name;
    prepare a way for him who rides on the
        clouds. *i*
    His name is the LORD—be glad in his
        presence!

5 God, who lives in his sacred Temple,
    cares for orphans and protects widows.
6 He gives the lonely a home to live in
    and leads prisoners out into happy freedom,
    but rebels will have to live in a desolate
        land.

7 O God, when you led your people,
    when you marched across the desert,

h HEBREW TITLE: *A psalm by David; a song.*   *i* on the clouds; *or* across the desert.

8 the earth shook, and the sky poured down
   rain,
   because of the coming of the God of
     Sinai,*j*
   the coming of the God of Israel.
9 You caused abundant rain to fall
   and restored your worn-out land;
10 your people made their home there;
   in your goodness you provided for the
     poor.

11 The Lord gave the command,
   and many women carried the news:
12 "Kings and their armies are running away!"
   The women at home divided what was
     captured:
13   figures of doves covered with silver,
   whose wings glittered with fine gold.
   (Why did some of you stay among the sheep
     pens on the day of battle?)
14 When Almighty God scattered the kings on
   Mount Zalmon,
   he caused snow to fall there.

15 What a mighty mountain is Bashan,
   a mountain of many peaks!
16 Why from your mighty peaks do you look
   with scorn
   on the mountain*k* on which God chose to
     live?
   The LORD will live there forever!

j GOD OF SINAI: *As the people of Israel went from Egypt to Canaan, God revealed himself to them at Mount Sinai (see Ex 19.16-25).*   *k* MOUNTAIN: *See 2.6.*

17 With his many thousands of mighty chariots
    the Lord comes from Sinai *l* into the holy
      place.
18 He goes up to the heights,
    taking many captives with him;
    he receives gifts from rebellious people.
The LORD God will live there.

19 Praise the Lord,
    who carries our burdens day after day;
    he is the God who saves us.
20 Our God is a God who saves;
    he is the LORD, our Lord,
    who rescues us from death.

21 God will surely break the heads of his
      enemies,
    of those who persist in their sinful ways.
22 The Lord has said, "I will bring your enemies
      back from Bashan;
    I will bring them back from the depths of
      the ocean,
23 so that you may wade in their blood,
    and your dogs may lap up as much as they
      want."

24 O God, your march of triumph is seen by all,
    the procession of God, my king, into his
      sanctuary.
25 The singers are in front, the musicians are
      behind,

l Probable text comes from Sinai; *Hebrew* in them, Sinai.

in between are the young women beating
the tambourines.
26 "Praise God in the meeting of his people;
praise the LORD, all you descendants of
Jacob!"
27 First comes Benjamin, the smallest tribe,
then the leaders of Judah with their group,
followed by the leaders of Zebulun and
Naphtali.

28 Show your power, O God,
the power you have used on our behalf
29   from your Temple in Jerusalem,
where kings bring gifts to you.
30 Rebuke Egypt, that wild animal in the reeds;
rebuke the nations, that herd of bulls with
their calves,
until they all bow down and offer you their
silver.
Scatter those people who love to make war!*m*
31 Ambassadors *n* will come from Egypt;
the Ethiopians*o* will raise their hands in
prayer to God.

32 Sing to God, kingdoms of the world,
sing praise to the Lord,
33   to him who rides in the sky,
the ancient sky.
Listen to him shout with a mighty roar.

---

m Verse 30 in Hebrew is unclear.   n Some ancient translations Ambassadors; *Hebrew
unclear.   o Hebrew* Cushites: *Cush is the ancient name of the extensive territory south
of the First Cataract of the Nile River. This region was called Ethiopia in
Graeco-Roman time, and included within its borders most of modern Sudan and some
of present-day Ethiopia (Abyssinia).*

34 Proclaim God's power;
    his majesty is over Israel,
    his might is in the skies.
35 How awesome is God as he comes from his
       sanctuary—
    the God of Israel!
He gives strength and power to his people.

Praise God!

A Cry for Help p

69 Save me, O God!
    The water is up to my neck;
2 I am sinking in deep mud,
    and there is no solid ground;
I am out in deep water,
    and the waves are about to drown me.
3 I am worn out from calling for help,
    and my throat is aching.
I have strained my eyes,
    looking for your help.

4 Those who hate me for no reason
    are more numerous than the hairs of my
      head.
My enemies tell lies against me;
    they are strong and want to kill me.
They made me give back things I did not
      steal.
5 My sins, O God, are not hidden from you;
    you know how foolish I have been.

p HEBREW TITLE: *By David.*

6 Don't let me bring shame on those who trust
  in you,
  Sovereign LORD Almighty!
 Don't let me bring disgrace to those who
  worship you,
  O God of Israel!
7 It is for your sake that I have been insulted
  and that I am covered with shame.
8 I am like a stranger to my relatives,
  like a foreigner to my family.

9 My devotion to your Temple burns in me like
  a fire;
  the insults which are hurled at you fall
  on me.
10 I humble myself*a* by fasting,
  and people insult me;
11 I dress myself in clothes of mourning,
  and they laugh at me.
12 They talk about me in the streets,
  and drunkards make up songs about me.

13 But as for me, I will pray to you, LORD;
  answer me, God, at a time you choose.
 Answer me because of your great love,
  because you keep your promise to save.
14 Save me from sinking in the mud;
  keep me safe from my enemies,
  safe from the deep water.
15 Don't let the flood come over me;
  don't let me drown in the depths

---

a Some ancient translations humble myself; *Hebrew* cry.

or sink into the grave.

16 Answer me, LORD, in the goodness of your
    constant love;
in your great compassion turn to me!
17 Don't hide yourself from your servant;
    I am in great trouble—answer me now!
18 Come to me and save me;
    rescue me from my enemies.

19 You know how I am insulted,
    how I am disgraced and dishonored;
    you see all my enemies.
20 Insults have broken my heart,
    and I am in despair.
  I had hoped for sympathy, but there was
      none;
    for comfort, but I found none.
21 When I was hungry, they gave me poison;
    when I was thirsty, they offered me
      vinegar.

22 May their banquets cause their ruin;
    may their sacred feasts cause their
      downfall.
23 Strike them with blindness!
    Make their backs always weak!
24 Pour out your anger on them;
    let your indignation overtake them.
25 May their camps be left deserted;
    may no one be left alive in their tents.
26 They persecute those whom you have
    punished;

they talk about the sufferings of those you
    have wounded.
27 Keep a record of all their sins;
    don't let them have any part in your
    salvation.
28 May their names be erased from the book of
    the living;
    may they not be included in the list of your
    people.

29 But I am in pain and despair;
    lift me up, O God, and save me!

30 I will praise God with a song;
    I will proclaim his greatness by giving him
    thanks.
31 This will please the LORD more than offering
    him cattle,
    more than sacrificing a full-grown bull.
32 When the oppressed see this, they will be
    glad;
    those who worship God will be encouraged.
33 The LORD listens to those in need
    and does not forget his people in prison.

34 Praise God, O heaven and earth,
    seas and all creatures in them.
35 He will save Jerusalem
    and rebuild the towns of Judah.
  His people will live there and possess the land;
36   the descendants of his servants will
      inherit it,
    and those who love him will live there.

A Prayer for Help[r]
(Psalm 40.13-17)

70 Save me, O God!
　　　Lord, help me now!
2 May those who try to kill me
　　be defeated and confused.
　May those who are happy because of my
　　　troubles
　　be turned back and disgraced.
3 May those who make fun of me
　　be dismayed by their defeat.

4 May all who come to you
　　be glad and joyful.
　May all who are thankful for your salvation
　　always say, "How great is God!"

5 I am weak and poor;
　　come to me quickly, O God.
　You are my savior and my Lord—
　　hurry to my aid!

The Prayer of an Elderly Person

71 Lord, I have come to you for protection;
　　　never let me be defeated!
2 Because you are righteous, help me and
　　　rescue me.
　　Listen to me and save me!
3 Be my secure shelter

[r] HEBREW TITLE: *A psalm by David; a lament.*

and a strong fortress[s] to protect me;
you are my refuge and defense.

4 My God, rescue me from wicked people,
from the power of cruel and evil people.
5 Sovereign LORD, I put my hope in you;
I have trusted in you since I was young.
6 I have relied on you all my life;
you have protected[t] me since the day I
was born.
I will always praise you.

7 My life has been an example to many,
because you have been my strong defender.
8 All day long I praise you
and proclaim your glory.
9 Do not reject me now that I am old;
do not abandon me now that I am feeble.
10 My enemies want to kill me;
they talk and plot against me.
11 They say, "God has abandoned him;
let's go after him and catch him;
there is no one to rescue him."

12 Don't stay so far away, O God;
my God, hurry to my aid!
13 May those who attack me
be defeated and destroyed.
May those who try to hurt me
be shamed and disgraced.
14 I will always put my hope in you;

---

[s] *One ancient translation* a strong fortress; *Hebrew* to go always you commanded.
[t] *Some ancient translations* protected; *Hebrew unclear.*

    I will praise you more and more.
15 I will tell of your goodness;
    all day long I will speak of your salvation,
    though it is more than I can understand.
16 I will go in the strength of the Lord God;
    I will proclaim your goodness, yours alone.

17 You have taught me ever since I was young,
    and I still tell of your wonderful acts.
18 Now that I am old and my hair is gray,
    do not abandon me, O God!
Be with me while I proclaim your power and
      might
    to all generations to come.

19 Your righteousness, God, reaches the skies.
    You have done great things;
    there is no one like you.
20 You have sent troubles and suffering on me,
    but you will restore my strength;
    you will keep me from the grave.
21 You will make me greater than ever;
    you will comfort me again.

22 I will indeed praise you with the harp;
    I will praise your faithfulness, my God.
On my harp I will play hymns to you,
    the Holy One of Israel.
23 I will shout for joy as I play for you;
    with my whole being I will sing
    because you have saved me.
24 I will speak of your righteousness all day
      long,

because those who tried to harm me
have been defeated and disgraced.

A Prayer for the King [u]

72 Teach the king to judge with your
righteousness, O God;
share with him your own justice,
2 so that he will rule over your people with
justice
and govern the oppressed with
righteousness.
3 May the land enjoy prosperity;
may it experience righteousness.
4 May the king judge the poor fairly;
may he help the needy
and defeat their oppressors.
5 May your people worship you as long as the
sun shines,
as long as the moon gives light, for ages to
come.

6 May the king be like rain on the fields,
like showers falling on the land.
7 May righteousness flourish in his lifetime,
and may prosperity last as long as the
moon gives light.

8 His kingdom will reach from sea to sea,
from the Euphrates to the ends of the
earth.

[u] HEBREW TITLE: *By Solomon.*

9 The peoples of the desert will bow down
        before him;
    his enemies will throw themselves to the
        ground.
10 The kings of Spain and of the islands will
        offer him gifts;
    the kings of Sheba and Seba[v] will bring
        him offerings.
11 All kings will bow down before him;
    all nations will serve him.

12 He rescues the poor who call to him,
    and those who are needy and neglected.
13 He has pity on the weak and poor;
    he saves the lives of those in need.
14 He rescues them from oppression and
        violence;
    their lives are precious to him.

15 Long live the king!
    May he be given gold from Sheba;[w]
    may prayers be said for him at all times;
    may God's blessings be on him always!
16 May there be plenty of grain in the land;
    may the hills be covered with crops,
        as fruitful as those of Lebanon.
    May the cities be filled with people,
        like fields full of grass.
17 May the king's name never be forgotten;
    may his fame last as long as the sun.
    May all nations ask God to bless them

[v] SHEBA AND SEBA: *Sheba was toward the south in Arabia and Seba was on the opposite side of the Red Sea.*   [w] SHEBA: *See 72.10.*

as he has blessed the king.*

18 Praise the LORD, the God of Israel!
  He alone does these wonderful things.
19 Praise his glorious name forever!
  May his glory fill the whole world.

Amen! Amen!

20 This is the end of the prayers of David son of
  Jesse.

BOOK THREE
(Psalms 73–89)

The Justice of God *y*

73 God is indeed good to Israel,
     to those who have pure hearts.
2 But I had nearly lost confidence;
  my faith was almost gone
3 because I was jealous of the proud
  when I saw that things go well for the
    wicked.

4 They do not suffer pain;
  they are strong and healthy.
5 They do not suffer as other people do;
  they do not have the troubles that others
    have.
6 And so they wear pride like a necklace
  and violence like a robe;

---

x as he has blessed the king; *or* and may they wish happiness for the king.
y HEBREW TITLE: *By Asaph.*

7 their hearts pour out evil, [z]
    and their minds are busy with wicked
        schemes.
8 They laugh at other people and speak of evil
        things;
    they are proud and make plans to oppress
        others.
9 They speak evil of God in heaven
    and give arrogant orders to everyone on
        earth,
10 so that even God's people turn to them
    and eagerly believe whatever they say. [a]
11 They say, "God will not know;
    the Most High will not find out."
12 That is what the wicked are like.
    They have plenty and are always getting
        more.

13 Is it for nothing, then, that I have kept myself
        pure
    and have not committed sin?
14 O God, you have made me suffer all day
        long;
    every morning you have punished me.

15 If I had said such things,
    I would not be acting as one of your
        people.
16 I tried to think this problem through,
    but it was too difficult for me
17   until I went into your Temple.

---

[z] *Some ancient translations* their hearts pour out evil; *Hebrew unclear.*   [a] *Verse 10 in Hebrew is unclear.*

Then I understood what will happen to the
    wicked.

18 You will put them in slippery places
    and make them fall to destruction!
19 They are instantly destroyed;
    they go down to a horrible end.
20 They are like a dream that goes away in the
    morning;
    when you rouse yourself, O Lord, they
    disappear.

21 When my thoughts were bitter
    and my feelings were hurt,
22 I was as stupid as an animal;
    I did not understand you.
23 Yet I always stay close to you,
    and you hold me by the hand.
24 You guide me with your instruction
    and at the end you will receive me with
    honor.
25 What else do I have in heaven but you?
    Since I have you, what else could I want
    on earth?
26 My mind and my body may grow weak,
    but God is my strength;
    he is all I ever need.

27 Those who abandon you will certainly perish;
    you will destroy those who are unfaithful
    to you.
28 But as for me, how wonderful to be
    near God,

to find protection with the Sovereign LORD
and to proclaim all that he has done!

A Prayer for National Deliverance [b]

74 Why have you abandoned us like this,
       O God?
Will you be angry with your own people
     forever?
2 Remember your people, whom you chose for
     yourself long ago,
whom you brought out of slavery to be
     your own tribe.
Remember Mount Zion, where once you
     lived.
3 Walk over these total ruins;
     our enemies have destroyed everything in
     the Temple.

4 Your enemies have shouted in triumph in
     your Temple;
they have placed their flags there as signs
     of victory.
5 They looked like woodsmen
     cutting down trees with their axes.[c]
6 They smashed all the wooden panels
     with their axes and sledge hammers.
7 They wrecked your Temple and set it on fire;
     they desecrated the place where you are
     worshiped.
8 They wanted to crush us completely;

[b] HEBREW TITLE: *A poem by Asaph.*   [c] *Verse 5 in Hebrew is unclear.*

they burned down every holy place in the
    land.

9 All our sacred symbols are gone;
    there are no prophets left,
    and no one knows how long this will last.
10 How long, O God, will our enemies laugh
      at you?
    Will they insult your name forever?
11 Why have you refused to help us?
    Why do you keep your hands behind you?*d*

12 But you have been our king from the
      beginning, O God;
    you have saved us many times.
13 With your mighty strength you divided the sea
    and smashed the heads of the sea monsters;
14 you crushed the heads of the monster
      Leviathan*e*
    and fed his body to desert animals.*f*
15 You made springs and fountains flow;
    you dried up large rivers.
16 You created the day and the night;
    you set the sun and the moon in their
      places;
17 you set the limits of the earth;
    you made summer and winter.

18 But remember, O LORD, that your enemies
    laugh at you,

d Probable text Why do you keep your hands behind you; *Hebrew unclear.*
e LEVIATHAN: *A legendary monster which was a symbol of the forces of chaos and evil.*
f animals; *or* people.

that they are godless and despise you.
19 Don't abandon your helpless people to their
    cruel enemies;
    don't forget your persecuted people!

20 Remember the covenant you made with us.
    There is violence in every dark corner of
        the land.
21 Don't let the oppressed be put to shame;
    let those poor and needy people praise you.

22 Rouse yourself, God, and defend your cause!
    Remember that godless people laugh at you
        all day long.
23 Don't forget the angry shouts of your
        enemies,
    the continuous noise made by your foes.

God the Judge [g]

75 We give thanks to you, O God, we give
        thanks to you!
    We proclaim how great you are
    and tell of [h] the wonderful things you have
        done.

2 "I have set a time for judgment," says God,
    "and I will judge with fairness.
3 Though every living creature tremble
    and the earth itself be shaken,
    I will keep its foundations firm.
4 I tell the wicked not to be arrogant;

[g] HEBREW TITLE: *A psalm by Asaph; a song.*   [h] *Some ancient translations* We proclaim
how great you are and tell of; *Hebrew* Your name is near and they tell of.

5   I tell them to stop their boasting."

6 Judgment does not come from the east or
        from the west,
    from the north or from the south; *i*
7 it is God who is the judge,
    condemning some and acquitting others.
8 The LORD holds a cup in his hand,
    filled with the strong wine of his anger.
 He pours it out, and all the wicked drink it;
    they drink it down to the last drop.

9 But I will never stop speaking of the God of
        Jacob
    or singing praises to him.
10 He will break the power of the wicked,
    but the power of the righteous will be
        increased.

God the Victor *j*

76 God is known in Judah;
        his name is honored in Israel.
2 He has his home in Jerusalem;
    he lives on Mount Zion.
3 There he broke the arrows of the enemy,
    their shields and swords, yes, all their
        weapons.

4 How glorious you are, O God!

i Probable text from the north or from the south; *Hebrew* from the wilderness of the
mountains.   *j* HEBREW TITLE: *A psalm by Asaph; a song.*

How majestic, as you return from the
　　mountains
where you defeated your foes.
5 Their brave soldiers have been stripped of all
　　they had
and now are sleeping the sleep of death;
all their strength and skill was useless.
6 When you threatened them, O God of Jacob,
the horses and their riders fell dead.

7 But you, LORD, are feared by all.
No one can stand in your presence
when you are angry.
8 You made your judgment known from
　　heaven;
the world was afraid and kept silent,
9 when you rose up to pronounce judgment,
to save all the oppressed on earth.

10 Human anger only results in more praise
　　for you;
those who survive the wars will keep your
　　festivals. k

11 Give the LORD your God what you
　　promised him;
bring gifts to him, all you nearby nations.
God makes everyone fear him;
12 　he humbles proud princes
and terrifies great kings.

k *One ancient translation* will keep your festivals; *verse 10 in Hebrew is unclear.*

Comfort in Time of Distress *l*

77 I cry aloud to God;
    I cry aloud, and he hears me.
2 In times of trouble I pray to the Lord;
    all night long I lift my hands in prayer,
    but I cannot find comfort.
3 When I think of God, I sigh;
    when I meditate, I feel discouraged.

4 He keeps me awake all night;
    I am so worried that I cannot speak.
5 I think of days gone by
    and remember years of long ago.
6 I spend the night in deep thought; *m*
    I meditate, and this is what I ask myself:
7 "Will the Lord always reject us?
    Will he never again be pleased with us?
8 Has he stopped loving us?
    Does his promise no longer stand?
9 Has God forgotten to be merciful?
    Has anger taken the place of his
        compassion?"
10 Then I said, "What hurts me most is this—
    that God is no longer powerful." *n*

11 I will remember your great deeds, LORD;
    I will recall the wonders you did in the
        past.
12 I will think about all that you have done;
    I will meditate on all your mighty acts.

l HEBREW TITLE: *A psalm by Asaph.*   *m Some ancient translations* deep thought; *Hebrew* song.   *n Verse 10 in Hebrew is unclear.*

13 Everything you do, O God, is holy.
　　No god is as great as you.
14 You are the God who works miracles;
　　you showed your might among the nations.
15 By your power you saved your people,
　　the descendants of Jacob and of Joseph.

16 When the waters saw you, O God, they were
　　afraid,
　　and the depths of the sea trembled.
17 The clouds poured down rain;
　　thunder crashed from the sky,
　　and lightning flashed in all directions.
18 The crash of your thunder rolled out,
　　and flashes of lightning lit up the world;
　　the earth trembled and shook.
19 You walked through the waves;
　　you crossed the deep sea,
　　but your footprints could not be seen.
20 You led your people like a shepherd,
　　with Moses and Aaron in charge.

God and His People *o*

78　　Listen, my people, to my teaching,
　　　　and pay attention to what I say.
2 I am going to use wise sayings
　　and explain mysteries from the past,
3 　things we have heard and known,
　　things that our ancestors told us.
4 We will not keep them from our children;
　　we will tell the next generation

o HEBREW TITLE: *A poem by Asaph.*

about the L<small>ORD</small>'s power and his great deeds
and the wonderful things he has done.

5 He gave laws to the people of Israel
and commandments to the descendants of
Jacob.
He instructed our ancestors
to teach his laws to their children,
6 so that the next generation might learn them
and in turn should tell their children.
7 In this way they also will put their trust
in God
and not forget what he has done,
but always obey his commandments.
8 They will not be like their ancestors,
a rebellious and disobedient people,
whose trust in God was never firm
and who did not remain faithful to him.

9 The Ephraimites, armed with bows and
arrows,
ran away on the day of battle.
10 They did not keep their covenant with God;
they refused to obey his law.
11 They forgot what he had done,
the miracles they had seen him perform.
12 While their ancestors watched, God
performed miracles
in the plain of Zoan in the land of Egypt.
13 He divided the sea and took them through it;
he made the waters stand like walls.
14 By day he led them with a cloud
and all night long with the light of a fire.

[15] He split rocks open in the desert
      and gave them water from the depths.
[16] He caused a stream to come out of the rock
      and made water flow like a river.

[17] But they continued to sin against God,
      and in the desert they rebelled against the
         Most High.
[18] They deliberately put God to the test
      by demanding the food they wanted.
[19] They spoke against God and said,
      "Can God supply food in the desert?
[20] It is true that he struck the rock,
      and water flowed out in a torrent;
   but can he also provide us with bread
      and give his people meat?"

[21] And so the LORD was angry when he heard
         them;
      he attacked his people with fire,
      and his anger against them grew,
[22] because they had no faith in him
      and did not believe that he would save
         them.
[23] But he spoke to the sky above
      and commanded its doors to open;
[24] he gave them grain from heaven,
      by sending down manna for them to eat.
[25] So they ate the food of angels,
      and God gave them all they wanted.
[26] He also caused the east wind to blow,
      and by his power he stirred up the south
         wind;

27 and to his people he sent down birds,
as many as the grains of sand on the shore;
28 they fell in the middle of the camp
all around the tents.
29 So the people ate and were satisfied;
God gave them what they wanted.
30 But they had not yet satisfied their craving
and were still eating,
31 when God became angry with them
and killed their strongest men,
the best young men of Israel.

32 In spite of all this the people kept sinning;
in spite of his miracles they did not
trust him.
33 So he ended their days like a breath
and their lives with sudden disaster.
34 Whenever he killed some of them,
the rest would turn to him;
they would repent and pray earnestly
to him.
35 They remembered that God was their
protector,
that the Almighty came to their aid.
36 But their words were all lies;
nothing they said was sincere.
37 They were not loyal to him;
they were not faithful to their covenant
with him.

38 But God was merciful to his people.
He forgave their sin
and did not destroy them.

Many times he held back his anger
and restrained his fury.
39 He remembered that they were only mortal
beings,
like a wind that blows by and is gone.

40 How often they rebelled against him in the
desert;
how many times they made him sad!
41 Again and again they put God to the test
and brought pain to the Holy God of Israel.
42 They forgot his great power
and the day when he saved them from their
enemies
43   and performed his mighty acts and miracles
in the plain of Zoan in the land of Egypt.
44 He turned the rivers into blood,
and the Egyptians had no water to drink.
45 He sent flies among them, that tormented
them,
and frogs that ruined their land.
46 He sent locusts to eat their crops
and to destroy their fields.
47 He killed their grapevines with hail
and their fig trees with frost.
48 He killed their cattle with hail
and their flocks with lightning.p
49 He caused them great distress
by pouring out his anger and fierce rage,
which came as messengers of death.
50 He did not restrain his anger

p hail . . . lightning; or terrible disease . . . deadly plague.

or spare their lives,
but killed them with a plague.
51 He killed the first-born sons
of all the families of Egypt.

52 Then he led his people out like a shepherd
and guided them through the desert.
53 He led them safely, and they were not afraid;
but the sea came rolling over their enemies.
54 He brought them to his holy land,
to the mountains which he himself
conquered.
55 He drove out the inhabitants as his people
advanced;
he divided their land among the tribes of
Israel
and gave their homes to his people.

56 But they rebelled against Almighty God
and put him to the test.
They did not obey his commandments,
57   but were rebellious and disloyal like their
ancestors,
unreliable as a crooked arrow.
58 They angered him with their heathen places of
worship,
and with their idols they made him furious.
59 God was angry when he saw it,
so he rejected his people completely.
60 He abandoned his tent in Shiloh,*q*
the home where he had lived among us.

q SHILOH: *The central place of worship for the people of Israel before the time of King David.*

61 He allowed our enemies to capture the
          Covenant Box,
     the symbol of his power and glory.
62 He was angry with his own people
     and let them be killed by their enemies.
63 Young men were killed in war,
     and young women had no one to marry.
64 Priests died by violence,
     and their widows were not allowed to
          mourn.

65 At last the Lord woke up as though from
          sleep;
     he was like a strong man excited by wine.
66 He drove his enemies back
     in lasting and shameful defeat.
67 But he rejected the descendants of Joseph;
     he did not select the tribe of Ephraim.
68 Instead he chose the tribe of Judah
     and Mount Zion, which he dearly loves.
69 There he built his Temple
     like his home in heaven;
   he made it firm like the earth itself,
     secure for all time.

70 He chose his servant David;
     he took him from the pastures,
71   where he looked after his flocks,
     and he made him king of Israel,
     the shepherd of the people of God.
72 David took care of them with unselfish
          devotion
     and led them with skill.

A Prayer for the Nation's Deliverance [r]

79 O God, the heathen have invaded your
land.
They have desecrated your holy Temple
and left Jerusalem in ruins.
2 They left the bodies of your people for the
vultures,
the bodies of your servants for wild animals
to eat.
3 They shed your people's blood like water;
blood flowed like water all through
Jerusalem,
and no one was left to bury the dead.
4 The surrounding nations insult us;
they laugh at us and mock us.

5 LORD, will you be angry with us forever?
Will your anger continue to burn like fire?
6 Turn your anger on the nations that do not
worship you,
on the people who do not pray to you.
7 For they have killed your people;
they have ruined your country.

8 Do not punish us for the sins of our
ancestors.
Have mercy on us now;
we have lost all hope.
9 Help us, O God, and save us;
rescue us and forgive our sins
for the sake of your own honor.

[r] HEBREW TITLE: *A psalm by Asaph.*

¹⁰ Why should the nations ask us,
    "Where is your God?"
  Let us see you punish the nations
    for shedding the blood of your servants.

¹¹ Listen to the groans of the prisoners,
    and by your great power free those who are
      condemned to die.
¹² Lord, pay the other nations back seven times
    for all the insults they have hurled at you.
¹³ Then we, your people, the sheep of your
      flock,
  will thank you forever
  and praise you for all time to come.

A Prayer for the Nation's Restoration ^s

80 Listen to us, O Shepherd of Israel;
    hear us, leader of your flock.
  Seated on your throne above the winged
      creatures,
² reveal yourself to the tribes of Ephraim,
    Benjamin, and Manasseh.
  Show us your strength;
    come and save us!

³ Bring us back, O God!
  Show us your mercy, and we will be saved!

⁴ How much longer, LORD God Almighty,
    will you be angry with your people's
      prayers?

^s HEBREW TITLE: *A psalm by Asaph; a testimony.*

5 You have given us sorrow to eat,
     a large cup of tears to drink.
6 You let the surrounding nations fight over our
        land;
     our enemies insult us.

7 Bring us back, Almighty God!
     Show us your mercy, and we will be saved!

8 You brought a grapevine out of Egypt;
     you drove out other nations and planted it
        in their land.
9 You cleared a place for it to grow;
     its roots went deep, and it spread out over
        the whole land.
10 It covered the hills with its shade;
     its branches overshadowed the giant cedars.
11 It extended its branches to the
        Mediterranean Sea
     and as far as the Euphrates River.
12 Why did you break down the fences
        around it?
     Now anyone passing by can steal its
        grapes;
13   wild hogs trample it down,
     and wild animals feed on it.

14 Turn to us, Almighty God!
     Look down from heaven at us;
     come and save your people!
15 Come and save this grapevine that you
        planted,
     this young vine you made grow so strong!

16 Our enemies have set it on fire and cut it
        down;
    look at them in anger and destroy them!
17 Preserve and protect the people you have
        chosen,
    the nation you made so strong.
18 We will never turn away from you again;
    keep us alive, and we will praise you.

19 Bring us back, LORD God Almighty.
    Show us your mercy, and we will be saved.

A Song for a Festival [t]

81 Shout for joy to God our defender;
        sing praise to the God of Jacob!
2 Start the music and beat the tambourines;
    play pleasant music on the harps and the
        lyres.
3 Blow the trumpet for the festival,
    when the moon is new and when the moon
        is full.
4 This is the law in Israel,
    an order from the God of Jacob.
5 He gave it to the people of Israel
    when he attacked the land of Egypt.

    I hear an unknown voice saying,
6 "I took the burdens off your backs;
    I let you put down your loads of bricks.
7 When you were in trouble, you called to me,
    and I saved you.

[t] HEBREW TITLE: *By Asaph.*

From my hiding place in the storm, I
    answered you.
I put you to the test at the springs of
    Meribah.
8 Listen, my people, to my warning;
    Israel, how I wish you would listen to me!
9 You must never worship another god.
10 I am the LORD your God,
    who brought you out of Egypt.
Open your mouth, and I will feed you.

11 "But my people would not listen to me;
    Israel would not obey me.
12 So I let them go their stubborn ways
    and do whatever they wanted.
13 How I wish my people would listen to me;
    how I wish they would obey me!
14 I would quickly defeat their enemies
    and conquer all their foes.
15 Those who hate me would bow in fear
      before me;
    their punishment would last forever.
16 But I would feed you with the finest wheat
    and satisfy you with wild honey."

God the Supreme Ruler [u]

82 God presides in the heavenly council;
    in the assembly of the gods he gives his
      decision:
2 "You must stop judging unjustly;

[u] HEBREW TITLE: *A psalm by Asaph.*

you must no longer be partial to the
    wicked!
3 Defend the rights of the poor and the
    orphans;
    be fair to the needy and the helpless.
4 Rescue them from the power of evil people.

5 "How ignorant you are! How stupid!
    You are completely corrupt,
    and justice has disappeared from the world.
6 'You are gods,' I said;
    'all of you are children of the Most High.'
7 But you will die like mortals;
    your life will end like that of any prince."

8 Come, O God, and rule the world;
    all the nations are yours.

A Prayer for the Defeat of Israel's Enemies [v]

83 O God, do not keep silent;
    do not be still, do not be quiet!
2 Look! Your enemies are in revolt,
    and those who hate you are rebelling.
3 They are making secret plans against your
    people;
    they are plotting against those you protect.
4 "Come," they say, "let us destroy their
    nation,
    so that Israel will be forgotten forever."

5 They agree on their plan

[v] HEBREW TITLE: *A psalm by Asaph; a song.*

and form an alliance against you:
6 the people of Edom and the Ishmaelites;
   the people of Moab and the Hagrites;
7 the people of Gebal, Ammon, and Amalek,
   and of Philistia and Tyre.
8 Assyria has also joined them
   as a strong ally of the Ammonites and
      Moabites, the descendants of Lot.

9 Do to them what you did to the Midianites,
   and to Sisera and Jabin at the Kishon
      River.
10 You defeated them at Endor,
   and their bodies rotted on the ground.
11 Do to their leaders what you did to Oreb and
      Zeeb;
   defeat all their rulers as you did Zebah and
      Zalmunna,
12 who said, "We will take for our own
   the land that belongs to God."

13 Scatter them like dust, O God,
   like straw blown away by the wind.
14 As fire burns the forest,
   as flames set the hills on fire,
15 chase them away with your storm
   and terrify them with your fierce winds.
16 Cover their faces with shame, O LORD,
   and make them acknowledge your power.
17 May they be defeated and terrified forever;
   may they die in complete disgrace.
18 May they know that you alone are the LORD,
   supreme ruler over all the earth.

Longing for God's House [w]

84 How I love your Temple, LORD Almighty!
² How I want to be there!
I long to be in the LORD's Temple.
With my whole being I sing for joy
to the living God.
³ Even the sparrows have built a nest,
and the swallows have their own home;
they keep their young near your altars,
LORD Almighty, my king and my God.
⁴ How happy are those who live in your
Temple,
always singing praise to you.

⁵ How happy are those whose strength comes
from you,
who are eager to make the pilgrimage to
Mount Zion.
⁶ As they pass through the dry valley of Baca,
it becomes a place of springs;
the autumn rain fills it with pools.
⁷ They grow stronger as they go;
they will see the God of gods on Zion.

⁸ Hear my prayer, LORD God Almighty.
Listen, O God of Jacob!
⁹ Bless our king, O God,
the king you have chosen.

¹⁰ One day spent in your Temple
is better than a thousand anywhere else;

[w] HEBREW TITLE: *A psalm by the clan of Korah.*

I would rather stand at the gate of the house
of my God
than live in the homes of the wicked.
11 The LORD is our protector and glorious king,
blessing us with kindness and honor.
He does not refuse any good thing
to those who do what is right.
12 LORD Almighty, how happy are those who
trust in you!

A Prayer for the Nation's Welfare [w]

85 LORD, you have been merciful to your
land;
you have made Israel prosperous again.
2 You have forgiven your people's sins
and pardoned all their wrongs.
3 You stopped being angry with them
and held back your furious rage.

4 Bring us back, O God our savior,
and stop being displeased with us!
5 Will you be angry with us forever?
Will your anger never cease?
6 Make us strong again,
and we, your people, will praise you.
7 Show us your constant love, O LORD,
and give us your saving help.

8 I am listening to what the LORD God is
saying;
he promises peace to us, his own people,

[w] HEBREW TITLE: *A psalm by the clan of Korah.*

if we do not go back to our foolish ways.
9 Surely he is ready to save those who
    honor him,
  and his saving presence will remain in our
    land.

10 Love and faithfulness will meet;
  righteousness and peace will embrace.
11 Human loyalty will reach up from the earth,
  and God's righteousness will look down
    from heaven.
12 The LORD will make us prosperous,
  and our land will produce rich harvests.
13 Righteousness will go before the LORD
  and prepare the path for him.

A Prayer for Help [x]

86 Listen to me, LORD, and answer me,
    for I am helpless and weak.
2 Save me from death, because I am loyal
    to you;
  save me, for I am your servant and I trust
    in you.

3 You are my God, so be merciful to me;
  I pray to you all day long.
4 Make your servant glad, O Lord,
  because my prayers go up to you.
5 You are good to us and forgiving,
    full of constant love for all who pray
    to you.

[x] HEBREW TITLE: *A prayer by David.*

6 Listen, LORD, to my prayer;
    hear my cries for help.
7 I call to you in times of trouble,
    because you answer my prayers.

8 There is no god like you, O Lord,
    not one has done what you have done.
9 All the nations that you have created
    will come and bow down to you;
    they will praise your greatness.
10 You are mighty and do wonderful things;
    you alone are God.

11 Teach me, LORD, what you want me to do,
    and I will obey you faithfully;
    teach me to serve you with complete
      devotion.
12 I will praise you with all my heart, O Lord
      my God;
    I will proclaim your greatness forever.
13 How great is your constant love for me!
    You have saved me from the grave itself.
14 Proud people are coming against me, O God;
    a cruel gang is trying to kill me—
    people who pay no attention to you.
15 But you, O Lord, are a merciful and
      loving God,
    always patient, always kind and faithful.
16 Turn to me and have mercy on me;
    strengthen me and save me,
    because I serve you just as my mother did.

17 Show me proof of your goodness, LORD;
    those who hate me will be ashamed
    when they see that you have given me
       comfort and help.

In Praise of Jerusalem *y*

87 The LORD built his city on the sacred
        hill; *z*
2   more than any other place in Israel
    he loves the city of Jerusalem.
3 Listen, city of God,
    to the wonderful things he says about you:

4 "I will include Egypt and Babylonia
    when I list the nations that obey me;
the people of Philistia, Tyre, and Ethiopia*a*
    I will number among the inhabitants of
       Jerusalem."

5 Of Zion it will be said
    that all nations belong there
    and that the Almighty will make her strong.
6 The LORD will write a list of the peoples
    and include them all as citizens of
       Jerusalem.
7 They dance and sing,
    "In Zion is the source of all our blessings."

y HEBREW TITLE: *A psalm by the clan of Korah; a song.*   *z* SACRED HILL: *See 2.6.*
a Hebrew Cush: *Cush is the ancient name of the extensive territory south of the First Cataract of the Nile River. This region was called Ethiopia in Graeco-Roman time, and included within its borders most of modern Sudan and some of present-day Ethiopia (Abyssinia).*

A Cry for Help [b]

88 LORD God, my savior, I cry out all day,
and at night I come before you.
2 Hear my prayer;
listen to my cry for help!

3 So many troubles have fallen on me
that I am close to death.
4 I am like all others who are about to die;
all my strength is gone. [c]
5 I am abandoned among the dead;
I am like the slain lying in their graves,
those you have forgotten completely,
who are beyond your help.
6 You have thrown me into the depths of the
tomb,
into the darkest and deepest pit.
7 Your anger lies heavy on me,
and I am crushed beneath its waves.

8 You have caused my friends to abandon me;
you have made me repulsive to them.
I am closed in and cannot escape;
9   my eyes are weak from suffering.
LORD, every day I call to you
and lift my hands to you in prayer.

10 Do you perform miracles for the dead?
Do they rise up and praise you?
11 Is your constant love spoken of in the grave

b HEBREW TITLE: *A psalm by the clan of Korah; a song. A poem by Heman the Ezrahite.*
c all my strength is gone; *or* there is no help for me.

or your faithfulness in the place of
destruction?
12 Are your miracles seen in that place of
darkness
or your goodness in the land of the
forgotten?

13 LORD, I call to you for help;
every morning I pray to you.
14 Why do you reject me, LORD?
Why do you turn away from me?
15 Ever since I was young, I have suffered and
been near death;
I am worn out[d] from the burden of your
punishments.
16 Your furious anger crushes me;
your terrible attacks destroy me.
17 All day long they surround me like a flood;
they close in on me from every side.
18 You have made even my closest friends
abandon me,
and darkness is my only companion.

A Hymn in Time of National Trouble [e]

89 O LORD, I will always sing of your
constant love;
I will proclaim your faithfulness forever.
2 I know that your love will last for all time,
that your faithfulness is as permanent as
the sky.

---

[d] Probable text I am worn out; Hebrew unclear.   [e] HEBREW TITLE: A poem by Ethan
the Ezrahite.

3 You said, "I have made a covenant with the
     man I chose;
  I have promised my servant David,
4 'A descendant of yours will always be king;
  I will preserve your dynasty forever.' "

5 The heavens sing of the wonderful things
     you do;
  the holy ones sing of your faithfulness,
     LORD.
6 No one in heaven is like you, LORD;
  none of the heavenly beings is your equal.
7 You are feared in the council of the holy
     ones;
  they all stand in awe of you.

8 LORD God Almighty, none is as mighty
     as you;
  in all things you are faithful, O LORD.
9 You rule over the powerful sea;
  you calm its angry waves.
10 You crushed the monster Rahab*f* and
     killed it;
  with your mighty strength you defeated
     your enemies.
11 Heaven is yours, the earth also;
  you made the world and everything in it.
12 You created the north and the south;
  Mount Tabor and Mount Hermon sing to
     you for joy.
13 How powerful you are!

f RAHAB: *A legendary sea monster which represented the forces of chaos and evil.*

How great is your strength!
14 Your kingdom is founded on righteousness
　　　and justice;
　　　love and faithfulness are shown in all
　　　you do.

15 How happy are the people who worship you
　　　with songs,
　　　who live in the light of your kindness!
16 Because of you they rejoice all day long,
　　　and they praise you for your goodness.
17 You give us great victories;
　　　in your love you make us triumphant.
18 You, O LORD, chose our protector;
　　　you, the Holy God of Israel, gave us our
　　　king.

God's Promise to David

19 In a vision long ago you said to your faithful
　　　servants,
　　　"I have given help to a famous soldier;
　　　I have given the throne to one I chose from
　　　the people.
20 I have made my servant David king
　　　by anointing him with holy oil.
21 My strength will always be with him,
　　　my power will make him strong.
22 His enemies will never succeed against him;
　　　the wicked will not defeat him.
23 I will crush his foes
　　　and kill everyone who hates him.
24 I will love him and be loyal to him;

I will make him always victorious.
25 I will extend his kingdom
    from the Mediterranean to the Euphrates
      River.
26 He will say to me,
    'You are my father and my God;
    you are my protector and savior.'
27 I will make him my first-born son,
    the greatest of all kings.
28 I will always keep my promise to him,
    and my covenant with him will last forever.
29 His dynasty will be as permanent as the sky;
    a descendant of his will always be king.

30 "But if his descendants disobey my law
    and do not live according to my commands,
31 if they disregard my instructions
    and do not keep my commandments,
32 then I will punish them for their sins;
    I will make them suffer for their wrongs.
33 But I will not stop loving David
    or fail to keep my promise to him.
34 I will not break my covenant with him
    or take back even one promise I made him.

35 "Once and for all I have promised by my holy
      name:
    I will never lie to David.
36 He will always have descendants,
    and I will watch over his kingdom as long
      as the sun shines.
37 It will be as permanent as the moon,
    that faithful witness in the sky."

Lament over the Defeat of the King

38 But you are angry with your chosen king;
    you have deserted and rejected him.
39 You have broken your covenant with your
      servant
    and thrown his crown in the dirt.
40 You have torn down the walls of his city
    and left his forts in ruins.
41 All who pass by steal his belongings;
    all his neighbors laugh at him.
42 You have given the victory to his enemies;
    you have made them all happy.
43 You have made his weapons useless
    and let him be defeated in battle.
44 You have taken away his royal scepter [g]
    and knocked his throne to the ground.
45 You have made him old before his time
    and covered him with disgrace.

A Prayer for Deliverance

46 LORD, will you hide yourself forever?
    How long will your anger burn like fire?
47 Remember how short my life is;
    remember that you created all of us mortal!
48 Who can live and never die?
    How can we humans keep ourselves from
      the grave?

49 Lord, where are the former proofs of your
      love?

[g] *Probable text* royal scepter; *Hebrew* purity.

Where are the promises you made to
    David?
50 Don't forget how I, your servant, am insulted,
    how I endure all the curses *h* of the
    heathen.
51 Your enemies insult your chosen king,
    O LORD!
They insult him wherever he goes.

52 Praise the LORD forever!

Amen! Amen!

BOOK FOUR
(Psalms 90–106)

Of God and Human Beings *i*

90 O Lord, you have always been our home.
2 Before you created the hills
or brought the world into being,
you were eternally God,
and will be God forever.

3 You tell us to return to what we were;
    you change us back to dust.
4 A thousand years to you are like one day;
    they are like yesterday, already gone,
    like a short hour in the night.
5 You carry us away like a flood;
    we last no longer than a dream.
We are like weeds that sprout in the morning,

h Probable text curses; *Hebrew* crowds.   *i* HEBREW TITLE: *A prayer by Moses, the man of God.*

6   that grow and burst into bloom,
       then dry up and die in the evening.

7 We are destroyed by your anger;
     we are terrified by your fury.
8 You place our sins before you,
     our secret sins where you can see them.

9 Our life is cut short by your anger;
     it fades away like a whisper.
10 Seventy years is all we have—
     eighty years, if we are strong;
   yet all they bring us is trouble and sorrow;
     life is soon over, and we are gone.

11 Who has felt the full power of your anger?
     Who knows what fear your fury can bring?
12 Teach us how short our life is,
     so that we may become wise.

13 How much longer will your anger last?
     Have pity, O LORD, on your servants!
14 Fill us each morning with your constant love,
     so that we may sing and be glad all our life.
15 Give us now as much happiness as the
          sadness you gave us
     during all our years of misery.
16 Let us, your servants, see your mighty deeds;
     let our descendants see your glorious might.
17 Lord our God, may your blessings be with us.
     Give us success in all we do!

God Our Protector

91 Whoever goes to the Lord for safety,
whoever remains under the protection of
the Almighty,

2 can say to him,
"You are my defender and protector.
You are my God; in you I trust."

3 He will keep you safe from all hidden dangers
and from all deadly diseases.

4 He will cover you with his wings;
you will be safe in his care;
his faithfulness will protect and defend you.

5 You need not fear any dangers at night
or sudden attacks during the day

6   or the plagues that strike in the dark
or the evils that kill in daylight.

7 A thousand may fall dead beside you,
ten thousand all around you,
but you will not be harmed.

8 You will look and see
how the wicked are punished.

9 You have made the Lord your[j] defender,
the Most High your protector,

10 and so no disaster will strike you,
no violence will come near your home.

11 God will put his angels in charge of you
to protect you wherever you go.

12 They will hold you up with their hands

[j] *Probable text* your; *Hebrew* my.

to keep you from hurting your feet on the
    stones.
13 You will trample down lions and snakes,
    fierce lions and poisonous snakes.

14 God says, "I will save those who love me
    and will protect those who acknowledge me
      as LORD.
15 When they call to me, I will answer them;
    when they are in trouble, I will be with
      them.
    I will rescue them and honor them.
16 I will reward them with long life;
    I will save them."

A Song of Praise k

92 How good it is to give thanks to you,
      O LORD,
    to sing in your honor, O Most High God,
2 to proclaim your constant love every morning
    and your faithfulness every night,
3 with the music of stringed instruments
    and with melody on the harp.
4 Your mighty deeds, O LORD, make me glad;
    because of what you have done, I sing
      for joy.

5 How great are your actions, LORD!
    How deep are your thoughts!
6 This is something a fool cannot know;
    someone who is stupid cannot understand:

k HEBREW TITLE: *A psalm; a song for the Sabbath.*

7 the wicked may grow like weeds,
   those who do wrong may prosper;
yet they will be totally destroyed,
8   because you, LORD, are supreme forever.

9 We know that your enemies will die,
   and all the wicked will be defeated.
10 You have made me as strong as a wild ox;
   you have blessed me with happiness.
11 I have seen the defeat of my enemies
   and heard the cries of the wicked.

12 The righteous will flourish like palm trees;
   they will grow like the cedars of Lebanon.
13 They are like trees planted in the house of the
      LORD,
   that flourish in the Temple of our God,
14   that still bear fruit in old age
   and are always green and strong.
15 This shows that the LORD is just,
   that there is no wrong in my protector.

God the King

93   The LORD is king.
         He is clothed with majesty and strength.
   The earth is set firmly in place
      and cannot be moved.
   2 Your throne, O LORD, has been firm from the
         beginning,
      and you existed before time began.

   3 The ocean depths raise their voice, O LORD;

they raise their voice and roar.
4 The LORD rules supreme in heaven,
      greater than the roar of the ocean,
      more powerful than the waves of the sea.

5 Your laws are eternal, LORD,
      and your Temple is holy indeed,
      forever and ever.

God the Judge of All

94 LORD, you are a God who punishes;
        reveal your anger!
2 You are the judge of us all;
      rise and give the proud what they deserve!
3 How much longer will the wicked be glad?
      How much longer, LORD?
4 How much longer will criminals be proud
      and boast about their crimes?

5 They crush your people, LORD;
      they oppress those who belong to you.
6 They kill widows and orphans,
      and murder the strangers who live in our
        land.
7 They say, "The LORD does not see us;
      the God of Israel does not notice."

8 My people, how can you be such stupid
        fools?
      When will you ever learn?
9 God made our ears—can't he hear?
      He made our eyes—can't he see?

¹⁰ He scolds the nations—won't he punish
      them?*ˡ*
   He is the teacher of us all—hasn't he any
      knowledge?
¹¹ The LORD knows what we think;
   he knows how senseless our reasoning is.

¹² LORD, how happy are those you instruct,
   the ones to whom you teach your law!
¹³ You give them rest from days of trouble
   until a pit is dug to trap the wicked.
¹⁴ The LORD will not abandon his people;
   he will not desert those who belong to him.
¹⁵ Justice will again be found in the courts,
   and all righteous people will support it.

¹⁶ Who stood up for me against the wicked?
   Who took my side against the evildoers?
¹⁷ If the LORD had not helped me,
   I would have gone quickly to the land of
      silence.*ᵐ*
¹⁸ I said, "I am falling";
   but your constant love, O LORD, held
      me up.
¹⁹ Whenever I am anxious and worried,
   you comfort me and make me glad.

²⁰ You have nothing to do with corrupt judges,
   who make injustice legal,
²¹   who plot against good people
   and sentence the innocent to death.

ˡ them?; *or* our wicked leaders?   *ᵐ* LAND OF SILENCE: *The world of the dead (see 6.5).*

22 But the LORD defends me;
    my God protects me.
23 He will punish them for their wickedness
    and destroy them for their sins;
    the LORD our God will destroy them.

A Song of Praise

95 Come, let us praise the LORD!
    Let us sing for joy to God, who
        protects us!
2 Let us come before him with thanksgiving
    and sing joyful songs of praise.
3 For the LORD is a mighty God,
    a mighty king over all the gods.
4 He rules over the whole earth,
    from the deepest caves to the highest hills.
5 He rules over the sea, which he made;
    the land also, which he himself formed.

6 Come, let us bow down and worship him;
    let us kneel before the LORD, our Maker!
7 He is our God;
    we are the people he cares for,
    the flock for which he provides.

    Listen today to what he says:
8 "Don't be stubborn, as your ancestors were at
        Meribah,
    as they were that day in the desert at
        Massah.
9 There they put me to the test and tried me,
    although they had seen what I did for them.

10 For forty years I was disgusted with those
    people.
    I said, 'How disloyal they are!
    They refuse to obey my commands.'
11 I was angry and made a solemn promise:
    'You will never enter the land
    where I would have given you rest.' "

God the Supreme King
(1 Chronicles 16.23-33)

96 Sing a new song to the Lord!
    Sing to the Lord, all the world!
2 Sing to the Lord, and praise him!
    Proclaim every day the good news that he
    has saved us.
3 Proclaim his glory to the nations,
    his mighty deeds to all peoples.

4 The Lord is great and is to be highly praised;
    he is to be honored more than all the gods.
5 The gods of all other nations are only idols,
    but the Lord created the heavens.
6 Glory and majesty surround him;
    power and beauty fill his Temple.

7 Praise the Lord, all people on earth;
    praise his glory and might.
8 Praise the Lord's glorious name;
    bring an offering and come into his Temple.
9 Bow down before the Holy One when he
    appears; [n]

[n] when he appears; or in garments of worship.

tremble before him, all the earth!

10 Say to all the nations, "The LORD is king!
    The earth is set firmly in place and cannot
        be moved;
    he will judge the peoples with justice."
11 Be glad, earth and sky!
    Roar, sea, and every creature in you;
12   be glad, fields, and everything in you!
    The trees in the woods will shout for joy
13   when the LORD comes to rule the earth.
    He will rule the peoples of the world
        with justice and fairness.

God the Supreme Ruler

97 The LORD is king! Earth, be glad!
        Rejoice, you islands of the seas!
2 Clouds and darkness surround him;
    he rules with righteousness and justice.
3 Fire goes in front of him
    and burns up his enemies around him.
4 His lightning lights up the world;
    the earth sees it and trembles.
5 The hills melt like wax before the LORD,
    before the Lord of all the earth.
6 The heavens proclaim his righteousness,
    and all the nations see his glory.

7 Everyone who worships idols is put to shame;
    all the gods bow down*o* before the LORD.
8 The people of Zion are glad,

o all the gods bow down; *or* bow down, all gods.

and the cities of Judah rejoice
因 because of your judgments, O Lord.
⁹ Lord Almighty, you are ruler of all the earth;
  you are much greater than all the gods.

¹⁰ The Lord loves those who hate evil; *p*
  he protects the lives of his people;
  he rescues them from the power of the
    wicked.
¹¹ Light shines on the righteous,
  and gladness on the good.
¹² All you that are righteous be glad
  because of what the Lord has done!
Remember what the holy God has done,
  and give thanks to him.

God the Ruler of the World *q*

98 Sing a new song to the Lord;
      he has done wonderful things!
By his own power and holy strength
  he has won the victory.
² The Lord announced his victory;
  he made his saving power known to the
    nations.
³ He kept his promise to the people of Israel
  with loyalty and constant love for them.
All people everywhere have seen the victory
  of our God.

⁴ Sing for joy to the Lord, all the earth;
  praise him with songs and shouts of joy!

p Probable text The Lord loves those who hate evil; *Hebrew* Hate evil, you who love
the Lord.   *q* HEBREW TITLE: *A psalm.*

5 Sing praises to the LORD!
    Play music on the harps!
6 Blow trumpets and horns,
    and shout for joy to the LORD, our king.

7 Roar, sea, and every creature in you;
    sing, earth, and all who live on you!
8 Clap your hands, you rivers;
    you hills, sing together with joy before the
       LORD,
9   because he comes to rule the earth.
He will rule the peoples of the world
    with justice and fairness.

God the Supreme King

99   The LORD is king,
    and the people tremble.
He sits on his throne above the winged
      creatures,
    and the earth shakes.
2 The LORD is mighty in Zion;
    he is supreme over all the nations.
3 Everyone will praise his great and majestic
      name.
    Holy is he!

4 Mighty king,[r] you love what is right;
    you have established justice in Israel;
    you have brought righteousness and
      fairness.
5 Praise the LORD our God;

r *Probable text* Mighty king; *Hebrew* The might of the king.

worship before his throne!
Holy is he!

6 Moses and Aaron were his priests,
    and Samuel was one who prayed to him;
    they called to the LORD, and he answered
        them.
7 He spoke to them from the pillar of cloud;
    they obeyed the laws and commands that
        he gave them.

8 O LORD, our God, you answered your people;
    you showed them that you are a God who
        forgives,
    even though you punished them for their
        sins.
9 Praise the LORD our God,
    and worship at his sacred hill! *s*
The LORD our God is holy.

A Hymn of Praise *t*

100 Sing to the LORD, all the world!
    2 Worship the LORD with joy;
    come before him with happy songs!

3 Acknowledge that the LORD is God.
    He made us, and we belong to him;
    we are his people, we are his flock.

4 Enter the Temple gates with thanksgiving;
    go into its courts with praise.

s SACRED HILL: *See 2.6.*   *t* HEBREW TITLE: *A psalm of thanksgiving.*

Give thanks to him and praise him.

5 The LORD is good;
    his love is eternal
    and his faithfulness lasts forever.

A King's Promise [u]

101 My song is about loyalty and justice,
        and I sing it to you, O LORD.
2 My conduct will be faultless.
    When will you come to me?

    I will live a pure life in my house
3   and will never tolerate evil.
    I hate the actions of those who turn away
        from God;
    I will have nothing to do with them.
4 I will not be dishonest[v]
    and will have no dealings with evil.[w]
5 I will get rid of anyone
    who whispers evil things about someone
        else;
    I will not tolerate anyone
    who is proud and arrogant.

6 I will approve of those who are faithful
        to God
    and will let them live in my palace.
Those who are completely honest
    will be allowed to serve me.

[u] HEBREW TITLE: *A psalm by David.*   [v] not be dishonest; *or* stay away from dishonest
people.   [w] evil; *or* evil people.

7 No liar will live in my palace;
  no hypocrite will remain in my presence.
8 Day after day I will destroy
  the wicked in our land;
I will expel all who are evil
  from the city of the LORD.

The Prayer of a Troubled Youth ˣ

102 Listen to my prayer, O LORD,
       and hear my cry for help!
2 When I am in trouble,
  don't turn away from me!
Listen to me,
  and answer me quickly when I call!

3 My life is disappearing like smoke;
  my body is burning like fire.
4 I am beaten down like dry grass;
  I have lost my desire for food.
5 I groan aloud;
  I am nothing but skin and bones.
6 I am like a wild bird in the desert,
  like an owl in abandoned ruins.
7 I lie awake;
  I am like a lonely bird on a housetop.
8 All day long my enemies insult me;
  those who mock me use my name in
    cursing.

9-10 Because of your anger and fury,
  ashes are my food,

ˣ HEBREW TITLE: *A prayer by a weary sufferer who pours out his complaints to the LORD.*

and my tears are mixed with my drink.
You picked me up and threw me away.
11 My life is like the evening shadows;
    I am like dry grass.

12 But you, O Lord, are king forever;
    all generations will remember you.
13 You will rise and take pity on Zion;
        the time has come to have mercy on her;
        this is the right time.
14 Your servants love her,
        even though she is destroyed;
    they have pity on her,
        even though she is in ruins.

15 The nations will fear the Lord;
        all the kings of the earth will fear his
            power.
16 When the Lord rebuilds Zion,
        he will reveal his greatness.
17 He will hear his forsaken people
        and listen to their prayer.

18 Write down for the coming generation what
        the Lord has done,
    so that people not yet born will praise him.
19 The Lord looked down from his holy place on
        high,
    he looked down from heaven to earth.
20 He heard the groans of prisoners
        and set free those who were condemned
            to die.
21 And so his name will be proclaimed in Zion,

and he will be praised in Jerusalem
22 when nations and kingdoms come together
and worship the LORD.

23 The LORD has made me weak while I am still
young;
he has shortened my life.
24 O God, do not take me away now
before I grow old.

O LORD, you live forever;
25 long ago you created the earth,
and with your own hands you made the
heavens.
26 They will disappear, but you will remain;
they will all wear out like clothes.
You will discard them like clothes,
and they will vanish.
27 But you are always the same,
and your life never ends.
28 Our children will live in safety,
and under your protection
their descendants will be secure.

The Love of God ͏ʸ

103
Praise the LORD, my soul!
All my being, praise his holy name!
2 Praise the LORD, my soul,
and do not forget how kind he is.
3 He forgives all my sins
and heals all my diseases.

ʸ HEBREW TITLE: By David.

4 He keeps me from the grave
   and blesses me with love and mercy.
5 He fills my life^z with good things,
   so that I stay young and strong like an
      eagle.

6 The Lord judges in favor of the oppressed
   and gives them their rights.
7 He revealed his plans to Moses
   and let the people of Israel see his mighty
      deeds.
8 The Lord is merciful and loving,
   slow to become angry and full of constant
      love.
9 He does not keep on rebuking;
   he is not angry forever.
10 He does not punish us as we deserve
   or repay us according to our sins and
      wrongs.
11 As high as the sky is above the earth,
   so great is his love for those who
      honor him.
12 As far as the east is from the west,
   so far does he remove our sins from us.
13 As a father is kind to his children,
   so the Lord is kind to those who
      honor him.
14 He knows what we are made of;
   he remembers that we are dust.

15 As for us, our life is like grass.

---

^z *Probable text* my life; *Hebrew unclear.*

We grow and flourish like a wild flower;
16   then the wind blows on it, and it is gone—
no one sees it again.
17 But for those who honor the LORD, his love
lasts forever,
and his goodness endures for all generations
18 of those who are true to his covenant
and who faithfully obey his commands.

19 The LORD placed his throne in heaven;
he is king over all.
20 Praise the LORD, you strong and mighty
angels,
who obey his commands,
who listen to what he says.
21 Praise the LORD, all you heavenly powers,
you servants of his, who do his will!
22 Praise the LORD, all his creatures
in all the places he rules.
Praise the LORD, my soul!

In Praise of the Creator

104 Praise the LORD, my soul!
O LORD, my God, how great you are!
You are clothed with majesty and glory;
2   you cover yourself with light.
You have spread out the heavens like a tent
3   and built your home on the waters above.[a]
You use the clouds as your chariot
and ride on the wings of the wind.
4 You use the winds as your messengers

---

[a] THE WATERS ABOVE: *A reference to the waters above the celestial dome (Gn 1.6, 7).*

and flashes of lightning as your servants.

5 You have set the earth firmly on its
        foundations,
    and it will never be moved.
6 You placed the ocean over it like a robe,
    and the water covered the mountains.
7 When you rebuked the waters, they fled;
    they rushed away when they heard your
        shout of command.
8 They flowed over the mountains and into the
        valleys,
    to the place you had made for them.
9 You set a boundary they can never pass,
    to keep them from covering the earth again.

10 You make springs flow in the valleys,
    and rivers run between the hills.
11 They provide water for the wild animals;
    there the wild donkeys quench their thirst.
12 In the trees near by,
    the birds make their nests and sing.

13 From the sky you send rain on the hills,
    and the earth is filled with your blessings.
14 You make grass grow for the cattle
    and plants for us to use,
  so that we can grow our crops
15   and produce wine to make us happy,
    olive oil to make us cheerful,
    and bread to give us strength.

16 The cedars of Lebanon get plenty of rain—

the LORD's own trees, which he planted.
17 There the birds build their nests;
the storks nest in the fir trees.
18 The wild goats live in the high mountains,
and the rock badgers hide in the cliffs.

19 You created the moon to mark the months;
the sun knows the time to set.
20 You made the night, and in the darkness
all the wild animals come out.
21 The young lions roar while they hunt,
looking for the food that God provides.
22 When the sun rises, they go back
and lie down in their dens.
23 Then people go out to do their work
and keep working until evening.

24 LORD, you have made so many things!
How wisely you made them all!
The earth is filled with your creatures.
25 There is the ocean, large and wide,
where countless creatures live,
large and small alike.
26 The ships sail on it, and in it plays Leviathan,
that sea monster which you made.*b*

27 All of them depend on you
to give them food when they need it.
28 You give it to them, and they eat it;
you provide food, and they are satisfied.
29 When you turn away, they are afraid;

b in it plays . . . made; *or* Leviathan is there, that sea monster you made to amuse you.

when you take away your breath, they die
and go back to the dust from which they
came.
30 But when you give them breath,[c] they are
created;
you give new life to the earth.

31 May the glory of the LORD last forever!
May the LORD be happy with what he has
made!
32 He looks at the earth, and it trembles;
he touches the mountains, and they pour
out smoke.

33 I will sing to the LORD all my life;
as long as I live I will sing praises to
my God.
34 May he be pleased with my song,
for my gladness comes from him.
35 May sinners be destroyed from the earth;
may the wicked be no more.

Praise the LORD, my soul!
Praise the LORD!

God and His People
(1 Chronicles 16.8-22)

105 Give thanks to the LORD, proclaim his
greatness;
tell the nations what he has done.
2 Sing praise to the LORD;

---

[c] give them breath; *or* send out your spirit.

tell the wonderful things he has done.
3 Be glad that we belong to him;
    let all who worship him rejoice.
4 Go to the LORD for help;
    and worship him continually.
5-6 You descendants of Abraham, his servant;
    you descendants of Jacob, the man he
        chose:
remember the miracles that God performed
    and the judgments that he gave.

7 The LORD is our God;
    his commands are for all the world.
8 He will keep his covenant forever,
    his promises for a thousand generations.
9 He will keep the agreement he made with
      Abraham
    and his promise to Isaac.
10 The LORD made a covenant with Jacob,
    one that will last forever.
11 "I will give you the land of Canaan," he said.
    "It will be your own possession."

12 God's people were few in number,
    strangers in the land of Canaan.
13 They wandered from country to country,
    from one kingdom to another.
14 But God let no one oppress them;
    to protect them, he warned the kings:
15 "Don't harm my chosen servants;
    do not touch my prophets."

16 The LORD sent famine to their country

and took away all their food.
¹⁷ But he sent a man ahead of them,
    Joseph, who had been sold as a slave.
¹⁸ His feet were kept in chains,
    and an iron collar was around his neck,
¹⁹   until what he had predicted came true.
The word of the LORD proved him right.
²⁰ Then the king of Egypt had him released;
    the ruler of nations set him free.
²¹ He put him in charge of his government
    and made him ruler over all the land,
²²   with power over the king's officials
    and authority to instruct his advisers.

²³ Then Jacob went to Egypt
    and settled in that country.
²⁴ The LORD gave many children to his people
    and made them stronger than their enemies.
²⁵ He made the Egyptians hate his people
    and treat his servants with deceit.

²⁶ Then he sent his servant Moses,
    and Aaron, whom he had chosen.
²⁷ They did God's mighty acts
    and performed miracles in Egypt.
²⁸ God sent darkness on the country,
    but the Egyptians did not obey ^d his
      command.
²⁹ He turned their rivers into blood
    and killed all their fish.
³⁰ Their country was overrun with frogs;

^d *Some ancient translations* did not obey; *Hebrew* obeyed.

even the palace was filled with them.
31 God commanded, and flies and gnats
    swarmed throughout the whole country.
32 He sent hail and lightning on their land
    instead of rain;
33 he destroyed their grapevines and fig trees
    and broke down all the trees.
34 He commanded, and the locusts came,
    countless millions of them;
35 they ate all the plants in the land;
    they ate all the crops.
36 He killed the first-born sons
    of all the families of Egypt.

37 Then he led the Israelites out;
    they carried silver and gold,
    and all of them were healthy and strong.
38 The Egyptians were afraid of them
    and were glad when they left.
39 God put a cloud over his people
    and a fire at night to give them light.
40 They [e] asked, and he sent quails;
    he gave them food from heaven to satisfy
      them.
41 He opened a rock, and water gushed out,
    flowing through the desert like a river.
42 He remembered his sacred promise
    to Abraham his servant.

43 So he led his chosen people out,
    and they sang and shouted for joy.

[e] *Some ancient translations* They; *Hebrew* He.

44 He gave them the lands of other peoples
  and let them take over their fields,
45 so that his people would obey his laws
  and keep all his commands.

Praise the LORD!

The LORD's Goodness to His People

106 Praise the LORD!

Give thanks to the LORD, because he is good;
  his love is eternal.
2 Who can tell all the great things he has done?
  Who can praise him enough?
3 Happy are those who obey his commands,
  who always do what is right.

4 Remember me, LORD, when you help your
    people;
  include me when you save them.
5 Let me see the prosperity of your people
  and share in the happiness of your nation,
  in the glad pride of those who belong
    to you.

6 We have sinned as our ancestors did;
  we have been wicked and evil.
7 Our ancestors in Egypt did not understand
    God's wonderful acts;
  they forgot the many times he showed them
    his love,

and they rebelled against the Almighty*f* at
    the Red Sea.
8 But he saved them, as he had promised,
    in order to show his great power.
9 He gave a command to the Red Sea,
    and it dried up;
    he led his people across on dry land.
10 He saved them from those who hated them;
    he rescued them from their enemies.
11 But the water drowned their enemies;
    not one of them was left.
12 Then his people believed his promises
    and sang praises to him.

13 But they quickly forgot what he had done
    and acted without waiting for his advice.
14 They were filled with craving in the desert
    and put God to the test;
15 so he gave them what they asked for,
    but also sent a terrible disease among them.

16 There in the desert they were jealous of
      Moses
    and of Aaron, the Lord's holy servant.
17 Then the earth opened up and swallowed
      Dathan
    and buried Abiram and his family;
18 fire came down on their followers
    and burned up those wicked people.

19 They made a gold bull-calf at Sinai

f Probable text the Almighty; *Hebrew* the sea.

and worshiped that idol;
20 they exchanged the glory of God
    for the image of an animal that eats grass.
21 They forgot the God who had saved them
    by his mighty acts in Egypt.
22 What wonderful things he did there!
    What amazing things at the Red Sea!
23 When God said that he would destroy his
      people,
    his chosen servant, Moses, stood up
      against God
    and kept his anger from destroying them.

24 Then they rejected the pleasant land,
    because they did not believe God's
      promise.
25 They stayed in their tents and grumbled
    and would not listen to the LORD.
26 So he gave them a solemn warning
    that he would make them die in the desert
27   and scatter their descendants among the
      heathen,
    letting them die in foreign countries.

28 Then at Peor, God's people joined in the
      worship of Baal
    and ate sacrifices offered to dead gods.
29 They stirred up the LORD's anger by their
      actions,
    and a terrible disease broke out among
      them.
30 But Phinehas stood up and punished the
      guilty,

and the plague was stopped.
31 This has been remembered in his favor ever
          since
and will be for all time to come.

32 At the springs of Meribah the people made
          the LORD angry,
     and Moses was in trouble on their account.
33 They made him so bitter
     that he spoke without stopping to think.

34 They did not kill the heathen,
     as the LORD had commanded them to do,
35 but they intermarried with them
     and adopted their pagan ways.
36 God's people worshiped idols,
     and this caused their destruction.
37 They offered their own sons and daughters
     as sacrifices to the idols of Canaan.
38 They killed those innocent children,
     and the land was defiled by those murders.
39 They made themselves impure by their
          actions
     and were unfaithful to God.

40 So the LORD was angry with his people;
     he was disgusted with them.
41 He abandoned them to the power of the
          heathen,
     and their enemies ruled over them.
42 They were oppressed by their enemies
     and were in complete subjection to them.
43 Many times the LORD rescued his people,

but they chose to rebel against him
and sank deeper into sin.
44 Yet the LORD heard them when they
cried out,
and he took notice of their distress.
45 For their sake he remembered his covenant,
and because of his great love he relented.
46 He made all their oppressors
feel sorry for them.

47 Save us, O LORD our God,
and bring us back from among the nations,
so that we may be thankful
and praise your holy name.

48 Praise the LORD, the God of Israel;
praise him now and forever!
Let everyone say, "Amen!"

Praise the LORD!

BOOK FIVE
(Psalms 107–150)

In Praise of God's Goodness

107 "Give thanks to the LORD, because he
is good;
his love is eternal!"
2 Repeat these words in praise to the LORD,
all you whom he has saved.
He has rescued you from your enemies

3   and has brought you back from foreign
           countries,
       from east and west, from north and south.*g*

4 Some wandered in the trackless desert
      and could not find their way to a city to
          live in.
5 They were hungry and thirsty
      and had given up all hope.
6 Then in their trouble they called to the LORD,
      and he saved them from their distress.
7 He led them by a straight road
      to a city where they could live.
8 They must thank the LORD for his constant
          love,
      for the wonderful things he did for them.
9 He satisfies those who are thirsty
      and fills the hungry with good things.

10 Some were living in gloom and darkness,
      prisoners suffering in chains,
11 because they had rebelled against the
          commands of Almighty God
      and had rejected his instructions.
12 They were worn out from hard work;
      they would fall down, and no one would
          help.
13 Then in their trouble they called to the LORD,
      and he saved them from their distress.
14 He brought them out of their gloom and
          darkness

g Probable text south; *Hebrew* the Mediterranean Sea *(meaning "west").*

and broke their chains in pieces.
15 They must thank the LORD for his constant
      love,
   for the wonderful things he did for them.
16 He breaks down doors of bronze
   and smashes iron bars.

17 Some were fools, suffering because of their
      sins
   and because of their evil;
18 they couldn't stand the sight of food
   and were close to death.
19 Then in their trouble they called to the LORD,
   and he saved them from their distress.
20 He healed them with his command
   and saved them from the grave.
21 They must thank the LORD for his constant
      love,
   for the wonderful things he did for them.
22 They must thank him with sacrifices,
   and with songs of joy must tell all that he
      has done.

23 Some sailed over the ocean in ships,
   earning their living on the seas.
24 They saw what the LORD can do,
   his wonderful acts on the seas.
25 He commanded, and a mighty wind began to
      blow
   and stirred up the waves.
26 The ships were lifted high in the air
   and plunged down into the depths.
   In such danger the sailors lost their courage;

27   they stumbled and staggered like drunks—
      all their skill was useless.
28 Then in their trouble they called to the LORD,
      and he saved them from their distress.
29 He calmed the raging storm,
      and the waves became quiet.
30 They were glad because of the calm,
      and he brought them safe to the port they
      wanted.
31 They must thank the LORD for his constant
      love,
      for the wonderful things he did for them.
32 They must proclaim his greatness in the
      assembly of the people
      and praise him before the council of the
      leaders.

33 The LORD made rivers dry up completely
      and stopped springs from flowing.
34 He made rich soil become a salty wasteland
      because of the wickedness of those who
      lived there.
35 He changed deserts into pools of water
      and dry land into flowing springs.
36 He let hungry people settle there,
      and they built a city to live in.
37 They sowed the fields and planted grapevines
      and reaped an abundant harvest.
38 He blessed his people, and they had many
      children;
      he kept their herds of cattle from
      decreasing.

³⁹ When God's people were defeated and
        humiliated
    by cruel oppression and suffering,
⁴⁰ he showed contempt for their oppressors
        and made them wander in trackless deserts.
⁴¹ But he rescued the needy from their misery
        and made their families increase like flocks.
⁴² The righteous see this and are glad,
        but all the wicked are put to silence.

⁴³ May those who are wise think about these
        things;
    may they consider the LORD's constant
        love.

A Prayer for Help against Enemies ʰ
(Psalm 57.7-11; 60.5-12)

108   I have complete confidence, O God!
        I will sing and praise you!
    Wake up, my soul!
²   Wake up, my harp and lyre!
        I will wake up the sun.
³ I will thank you, O LORD, among the nations.
        I will praise you among the peoples.
⁴ Your constant love reaches above the
        heavens;
    your faithfulness touches the skies.

⁵ Show your greatness in the sky, O God,
        and your glory over all the earth.
⁶ Save us by your might; answer my prayer,

ʰ HEBREW TITLE: *A psalm by David; a song.*

so that the people you love may be
rescued.

7 From his sanctuary [i] God has said,
"In triumph I will divide Shechem
and distribute Sukkoth Valley to my people.
8 Gilead is mine, and Manasseh too;
Ephraim is my helmet
and Judah my royal scepter.
9 But I will use Moab as my washbowl,
and I will throw my sandals on Edom,
as a sign that I own it.
I will shout in triumph over the Philistines."

10 Who, O God, will take me into the fortified
city?
Who will lead me to Edom?
11 Have you really rejected us?
Aren't you going to march out with our
armies?
12 Help us against the enemy;
human help is worthless.
13 With God on our side we will win;
he will defeat our enemies.

The Complaint of Someone in Trouble [j]

109 I praise you, God; don't remain silent!
2 Wicked people and liars have
attacked me.
They tell lies about me,
3 and they say evil things about me,

---

[i] From his sanctuary; or In his holiness.   [j] HEBREW TITLE: A psalm by David.

attacking me for no reason.
⁴ They oppose me, even though I love them
and have prayed for them.ᵏ
⁵ They pay me back evil for good
and hatred for love.

⁶ Choose some corrupt judge to try my enemy,
and let one of his own enemies accuse him.
⁷ May he be tried and found guilty;
may even his prayer be considered a crime!
⁸ May his life soon be ended;
may someone else take his job!
⁹ May his children become orphans,
and his wife a widow!
¹⁰ May his children be homeless beggars;
may they be driven fromˡ the ruins they
live in!
¹¹ May his creditors take away all his property,
and may strangers get everything he
worked for.
¹² May no one ever be kind to him
or care for the orphans he leaves behind.
¹³ May all his descendants die,
and may his name be forgotten in the next
generation.
¹⁴ May the LORD remember the evil of his
ancestors
and never forgive his mother's sins.
¹⁵ May the LORD always remember their sins,
but may they themselves be completely
forgotten!

ᵏ *Probable text* have prayed for them; *Hebrew unclear.*   ˡ *One ancient translation* be
driven from; *Hebrew* seek.

16 That man never thought of being kind;
    he persecuted and killed
    the poor, the needy, and the helpless.
17 He loved to curse—may he be cursed!
    He hated to give blessings—may no one
        bless him!
18 He cursed as naturally as he dressed himself;
    may his own curses soak into his body like
        water
    and into his bones like oil!
19 May they cover him like clothes
    and always be around him like a belt!

20 LORD, punish my enemies in that way—
    those who say such evil things against me!
21 But my Sovereign LORD, help me as you have
        promised,
    and rescue me because of the goodness of
        your love.
22 I am poor and needy;
    I am hurt to the depths of my heart.
23 Like an evening shadow I am about to vanish;
    I am blown away like an insect.
24 My knees are weak from lack of food;
    I am nothing but skin and bones.
25 When people see me, they laugh at me;
    they shake their heads in scorn.

26 Help me, O LORD my God;
    because of your constant love, save me!
27 Make my enemies know
    that you are the one who saves me.
28 They may curse me, but you will bless me.

May my persecutors be defeated,*m*
and may I, your servant, be glad.
29 May my enemies be covered with disgrace;
may they wear their shame like a robe.

30 I will give loud thanks to the LORD;
I will praise him in the assembly of the
people,
31 because he defends the poor
and saves them from those who condemn
them to death.

The LORD and His Chosen King *n*

110 The LORD said to my lord,
"Sit here at my right side
until I put your enemies under your feet."
2 From Zion the LORD will extend your royal
power.
"Rule over your enemies," he says.
3 On the day you fight your enemies,
your people will volunteer.
Like the dew of early morning
your young men will come to you on the
sacred hills.*o*

4 The LORD made a solemn promise and will
not take it back:
"You will be a priest forever
in the priestly order of Melchizedek."*p*

---

m One ancient translation May my persecutors be defeated; *Hebrew* They persecuted
me and were defeated.   *n* HEBREW TITLE: *A psalm by David.*   *o Verse 3 in Hebrew is*
unclear.   *p* in the priestly order of Melchizedek; *or* like Melchizedek; *or* in the line of
succession to Melchizedek.

5 The Lord is at your right side;
    when he becomes angry, he will defeat
      kings.
6 He will pass judgment on the nations
    and fill the battlefield with corpses;
    he will defeat kings all over the earth.
7 The king will drink from the stream by the
      road,
    and strengthened, he will stand victorious.

In Praise of the LORD

111 Praise the LORD!

With all my heart I will thank the LORD
    in the assembly of his people.
2 How wonderful are the things the LORD does!
    All who are delighted with them want to
      understand them.
3 All he does is full of honor and majesty;
    his righteousness is eternal.

4 The LORD does not let us forget his wonderful
      actions;
    he is kind and merciful.
5 He provides food for those who honor him;
    he never forgets his covenant.
6 He has shown his power to his people
    by giving them the lands of foreigners.

7 In all he does he is faithful and just;
    all his commands are dependable.
8 They last for all time;

they were given in truth and righteousness.
9 He set his people free
   and made an eternal covenant with them.
   Holy and mighty is he!
10 The way to become wise is to honor the
      LORD; *q*
   he gives sound judgment to all who obey
      his commands.
He is to be praised forever.

The Happiness of a Good Person

112   Praise the LORD!

Happy is the person who honors the LORD,
   who takes pleasure in obeying his
      commands.
2 The good man's children will be powerful in
      the land;
   his descendants will be blessed.
3 His family will be wealthy and rich,
   and he will be prosperous forever.

4 Light shines in the darkness for good people,
   for those who are merciful, kind, and just.
5 Happy is the person who is generous with his
      loans,
   who runs his business honestly.
6 A good person will never fail;
   he will always be remembered.

7 He is not afraid of receiving bad news;

q The way . . . the LORD; *or* The most important part of wisdom is honoring the LORD.

his faith is strong, and he trusts in the
    LORD.
8 He is not worried or afraid;
    he is certain to see his enemies defeated.
9 He gives generously to the needy,
    and his kindness never fails;
    he will be powerful and respected.
10 The wicked see this and are angry;
    they glare in hate and disappear;
    their hopes are gone forever.

In Praise of the LORD's Goodness

113 Praise the LORD!

You servants of the LORD,
    praise his name!
2 May his name be praised,
    now and forever.
3 From the east to the west
    praise the name of the LORD!
4 The LORD rules over all nations;
    his glory is above the heavens.

5 There is no one like the LORD our God.
He lives in the heights above,
6   but he bends down
    to see the heavens and the earth.
7 He raises the poor from the dust;
    he lifts the needy from their misery

⁸ and makes them companions of princes,
　　the princes of his people.
⁹ He honors the childless wife in her home;
　　he makes her happy by giving her children.

Praise the LORD!

A Passover Song

114 When the people of Israel left Egypt,
　　　　when Jacob's descendants left that
　　　　foreign land,
² Judah became the Lord's holy people,
　　Israel became his own possession.

³ The Red Sea looked and ran away;
　　the Jordan River stopped flowing.
⁴ The mountains skipped like goats;
　　the hills jumped around like lambs.

⁵ What happened, Sea, to make you run away?
　　And you, O Jordan, why did you stop
　　　　flowing?
⁶ You mountains, why did you skip like goats?
　　You hills, why did you jump around like
　　　　lambs?

⁷ Tremble, earth, at the Lord's coming,
　　at the presence of the God of Jacob,
⁸ who changes rocks into pools of water
　　and solid cliffs into flowing springs.

The One True God

115 To you alone, O LORD, to you alone,
and not to us, must glory be given
because of your constant love and
faithfulness.

2 Why should the nations ask us,
"Where is your God?"
3 Our God is in heaven;
he does whatever he wishes.
4 Their gods are made of silver and gold,
formed by human hands.
5 They have mouths, but cannot speak,
and eyes, but cannot see.
6 They have ears, but cannot hear,
and noses, but cannot smell.
7 They have hands, but cannot feel,
and feet, but cannot walk;
they cannot make a sound.
8 May all who made them and who trust in
them
become *r* like the idols they have made.

9 Trust in the LORD, you people of Israel.
He helps you and protects you.
10 Trust in the LORD, you priests of God.
He helps you and protects you.
11 Trust in the LORD, all you that worship him.
He helps you and protects you.

12 The LORD remembers us and will bless us;

r May all . . . become; *or* All who made them and who trust in them will become.

he will bless the people of Israel
and all the priests of God.
13 He will bless everyone who honors him,
the great and the small alike.

14 May the LORD give you children—
you and your descendants!
15 May you be blessed by the LORD,
who made heaven and earth!

16 Heaven belongs to the LORD alone,
but he gave the earth to us humans.
17 The LORD is not praised by the dead,
by any who go down to the land of
silence.*s*
18 But we, the living, will give thanks to him
now and forever.

Praise the LORD!

Someone Saved from Death Praises God

116 I love the LORD, because he hears me;
he listens to my prayers.
2 He listens to me
every time I call to him.
3 The danger of death was all around me;
the horrors of the grave closed in on me;
I was filled with fear and anxiety.
4 Then I called to the LORD,
"I beg you, LORD, save me!"

s LAND OF SILENCE: *The world of the dead (see 6.5).*

⁵ The Lᴏʀᴅ is merciful and good;
  our God is compassionate.
⁶ The Lᴏʀᴅ protects the helpless;
  when I was in danger, he saved me.
⁷ Be confident, my heart,
  because the Lᴏʀᴅ has been good to me.

⁸ The Lᴏʀᴅ saved me from death;
  he stopped my tears
  and kept me from defeat.
⁹ And so I walk in the presence of the Lᴏʀᴅ
  in the world of the living.
¹⁰ I kept on believing, even when I said,
  "I am completely crushed,"
¹¹ even when I was afraid and said,
  "No one can be trusted."

¹² What can I offer the Lᴏʀᴅ
  for all his goodness to me?
¹³ I will bring a wine offering to the Lᴏʀᴅ,
  to thank him for saving me.
¹⁴ In the assembly of all his people
  I will give him what I have promised.

¹⁵ How painful it is to the Lᴏʀᴅ
  when one of his people dies!
¹⁶ I am your servant, Lᴏʀᴅ;
  I serve you just as my mother did.
  You have saved me from death.
¹⁷ I will give you a sacrifice of thanksgiving
  and offer my prayer to you.
¹⁸⁻¹⁹ In the assembly of all your people,

in the sanctuary of your Temple in
    Jerusalem,
I will give you what I have promised.

Praise the LORD!

In Praise of the LORD

117 Praise the LORD, all nations!
        Praise him, all peoples!
² His love for us is strong,
    and his faithfulness is eternal.

Praise the LORD!

A Prayer of Thanks for Victory

118 Give thanks to the LORD, because he is
        good,
    and his love is eternal.
² Let the people of Israel say,
    "His love is eternal."
³ Let the priests of God say,
    "His love is eternal."
⁴ Let all who worship him say,
    "His love is eternal."

⁵ In my distress I called to the LORD;
    he answered me and set me free.
⁶ The LORD is with me, I will not be afraid;
    what can anyone do to me?
⁷ It is the LORD who helps me,
    and I will see my enemies defeated.

8 It is better to trust in the LORD
    than to depend on people.
9 It is better to trust in the LORD
    than to depend on human leaders.

10 Many enemies were around me;
    but I destroyed them by the power of the
      LORD!
11 They were around me on every side;
    but I destroyed them by the power of the
      LORD!
12 They swarmed around me like bees,
    but they burned out as quickly as a brush
      fire;
    by the power of the LORD I destroyed them.
13 I was fiercely attacked and was being
      defeated,
    but the LORD helped me.
14 The LORD makes me powerful and strong;
    he has saved me.

15 Listen to the glad shouts of victory in the
      tents of God's people:
    "The LORD's mighty power has done it!
16   His power has brought us victory—
    his mighty power in battle!"

17 I will not die; instead, I will live
    and proclaim what the LORD has done.
18 He has punished me severely,
    but he has not let me die.

¹⁹ Open to me the gates of the Temple;
    I will go in and give thanks to the LORD!

²⁰ This is the gate of the LORD;
    only the righteous can come in.

²¹ I praise you, LORD, because you heard me,
    because you have given me victory.

²² The stone which the builders rejected as
      worthless
    turned out to be the most important of all.
²³ This was done by the LORD;
    what a wonderful sight it is!
²⁴ This is the day of the LORD's victory;
    let us be happy, let us celebrate!
²⁵ Save us, LORD, save us!
    Give us success, O LORD!

²⁶ May God bless the one who comes in the
      name of the LORD!
    From the Temple of the LORD we
      bless you.
²⁷ The LORD is God; he has been good to us.
With branches in your hands, start the festival
    and march around the altar.

²⁸ You are my God, and I give you thanks;
    I will proclaim your greatness.

²⁹ Give thanks to the LORD, because he is good,
    and his love is eternal.

The Law of the LORD

119 Happy are those whose lives are
faultless,
who live according to the law of the LORD.
2 Happy are those who follow his commands,
who obey him with all their heart.
3 They never do wrong;
they walk in the LORD's ways.
4 LORD, you have given us your laws
and told us to obey them faithfully.
5 How I hope that I shall be faithful
in keeping your instructions!
6 If I pay attention to all your commands,
then I will not be put to shame.
7 As I learn your righteous judgments,
I will praise you with a pure heart.
8 I will obey your laws;
never abandon me!

Obedience to the Law of the LORD

9 How can young people keep their lives pure?
By obeying your commands.
10 With all my heart I try to serve you;
keep me from disobeying your
commandments.
11 I keep your law in my heart,
so that I will not sin against you.
12 I praise you, O LORD;
teach me your ways.
13 I will repeat aloud
all the laws you have given.
14 I delight in following your commands

more than in having great wealth.
15 I study your instructions;
     I examine your teachings.
16 I take pleasure in your laws;
     your commands I will not forget.

Happiness in the Law of the Lord

17 Be good to me, your servant,
     so that I may live and obey your teachings.
18 Open my eyes, so that I may see
     the wonderful truths in your law.
19 I am here on earth for just a little while;
     do not hide your commands from me.
20 My heart aches with longing;
     I want to know your judgments at all times.
21 You reprimand the proud;
     cursed are those who disobey your
          commands.
22 Free me from their insults and scorn,
     because I have kept your laws.
23 The rulers meet and plot against me,
     but I will study your teachings.
24 Your instructions give me pleasure;
     they are my advisers.

Determination to Obey the Law of the Lord

25 I lie defeated in the dust;
     revive me, as you have promised.
26 I confessed all I have done, and you
          answered me;
     teach me your ways.
27 Help me to understand your laws,

and I will meditate on your wonderful
  teachings.*

28 I am overcome by sorrow;
  strengthen me, as you have promised.
29 Keep me from going the wrong way,
  and in your goodness teach me your law.
30 I have chosen to be obedient;
  I have paid attention to your judgments.
31 I have followed your instructions, LORD;
  don't let me be put to shame.
32 I will eagerly obey your commands,
  because you will give me more
    understanding.

A Prayer for Understanding

33 Teach me, LORD, the meaning of your laws,
  and I will obey them at all times.
34 Explain your law to me, and I will obey it;
  I will keep it with all my heart.
35 Keep me obedient to your commandments,
  because in them I find happiness.
36 Give me the desire to obey your laws
  rather than to get rich.
37 Keep me from paying attention to what is
    worthless;
  be good to me, as you have promised.
38 Keep your promise to me, your servant—
  the promise you make to those who
    obey you.
39 Save me from the insults I fear;
  how wonderful are your judgments!

*teachings; *or* deeds.

⁴⁰ I want to obey your commands;
    give me new life, for you are righteous.

Trusting the Law of the LORD

⁴¹ Show me how much you love me, LORD,
    and save me according to your promise.
⁴² Then I can answer those who insult me
    because I trust in your word.
⁴³ Enable me to speak the truth at all times,
    because my hope is in your judgments.
⁴⁴ I will always obey your law,
    forever and ever.
⁴⁵ I will live in perfect freedom,
    because I try to obey your teachings.
⁴⁶ I will announce your commands to kings
    and I will not be ashamed.
⁴⁷ I find pleasure in obeying your commands,
    because I love them.
⁴⁸ I respect and love your commandments;
    I will meditate on your instructions.

Confidence in the Law of the LORD

⁴⁹ Remember your promise to me, your servant;
    it has given me hope.
⁵⁰ Even in my suffering I was comforted
    because your promise gave me life.
⁵¹ The proud are always scornful of me,
    but I have not departed from your law.
⁵² I remember your judgments of long ago,
    and they bring me comfort, O LORD.
⁵³ When I see the wicked breaking your law,
    I am filled with anger.

54 During my brief earthly life
  I compose songs about your commands.
55 In the night I remember you, LORD,
  and I think about your law.
56 I find my happiness
  in obeying your commands.

Devotion to the Law of the LORD

57 You are all I want, O LORD;
  I promise to obey your laws.
58 I ask you with all my heart
  to have mercy on me, as you have
    promised!
59 I have considered my conduct,
  and I promise to follow your instructions.
60 Without delay I hurry
  to obey your commands.
61 The wicked have laid a trap for me,
  but I do not forget your law.
62 In the middle of the night I wake up
  to praise you for your righteous judgments.
63 I am a friend of all who serve you,
  of all who obey your laws.
64 LORD, the earth is full of your constant love;
  teach me your commandments.

The Value of the Law of the LORD

65 You have kept your promise, LORD,
  and you are good to me, your servant.
66 Give me wisdom and knowledge,
  because I trust in your commands.
67 Before you punished me, I used to go wrong,

but now I obey your word.
68 How good you are—how kind!
Teach me your commands.
69 The proud have told lies about me,
but with all my heart I obey your
instructions.
70 They have no understanding,
but I find pleasure in your law.
71 My punishment was good for me,
because it made me learn your commands.
72 The law that you gave means more to me
than all the money in the world.

The Justice of the Law of the Lord

73 You created me, and you keep me safe;
give me understanding, so that I may learn
your laws.
74 Those who honor you will be glad when they
see me,
because I trust in your promise.
75 I know that your judgments are righteous,
Lord,
and that you punished me because you are
faithful.
76 Let your constant love comfort me,
as you have promised me, your servant.
77 Have mercy on me, and I will live
because I take pleasure in your law.
78 May the proud be ashamed for falsely
accusing me;
as for me, I will meditate on your
instructions.

⁷⁹ May those who honor you come to me—
    all those who know your commands.
⁸⁰ May I perfectly obey your commandments
    and be spared the shame of defeat.

A Prayer for Deliverance

⁸¹ I am worn out, LORD, waiting for you to
    save me;
    I place my trust in your word.
⁸² My eyes are tired from watching for what you
    promised,
    while I ask, "When will you help me?"
⁸³ I am as useless as a discarded wineskin;
    yet I have not forgotten your commands.
⁸⁴ How much longer must I wait?
    When will you punish those who
    persecute me?
⁸⁵ The proud, who do not obey your law,
    have dug pits to trap me.
⁸⁶ Your commandments are all trustworthy;
    people persecute me with lies—help me!
⁸⁷ They have almost succeeded in killing me,
    but I have not neglected your commands.
⁸⁸ Because of your constant love be good to me,
    so that I may obey your laws.

Faith in the Law of the LORD

⁸⁹ Your word, O LORD, will last forever;
    it is eternal in heaven.
⁹⁰ Your faithfulness endures through all the
    ages;

you have set the earth in place, and it
  remains.
91 All things remain to this day because of your
  command,
    because they are all your servants.
92 If your law had not been the source of
    my joy,
    I would have died from my sufferings.
93 I will never neglect your instructions,
    because by them you have kept me alive.
94 I am yours—save me!
    I have tried to obey your commands.
95 The wicked are waiting to kill me,
    but I will meditate on your laws.
96 I have learned that everything has limits;
    but your commandment is perfect.

Love for the Law of the Lord

97 How I love your law!
    I think about it all day long.
98 Your commandment is with me all the time
    and makes me wiser than my enemies.
99 I understand more than all my teachers,
    because I meditate on your instructions.
100 I have greater wisdom than those who
    are old,
    because I obey your commands.
101 I have avoided all evil conduct,
    because I want to obey your word.
102 I have not neglected your instructions,
    because you yourself are my teacher.
103 How sweet is the taste of your instructions—

sweeter even than honey!
104 I gain wisdom from your laws,
  and so I hate all bad conduct.

Light from the Law of the LORD

105 Your word is a lamp to guide me
  and a light for my path.
106 I will keep my solemn promise
  to obey your just instructions.
107 My sufferings, LORD, are terrible indeed;
  keep me alive, as you have promised.
108 Accept my prayer of thanks, O LORD,
  and teach me your commands.
109 I am always ready to risk my life;
  I*u* have not forgotten your law.
110 The wicked lay a trap for me,
  but I have not disobeyed your commands.
111 Your commandments are my eternal
    possession;
  they are the joy of my heart.
112 I have decided to obey your laws
  until the day I die.

Safety in the Law of the LORD

113 I hate those who are not completely loyal
    to you,
  but I love your law.
114 You are my defender and protector;
  I put my hope in your promise.

---

u I am always ready to risk my life; I; *or* My life is in constant danger, but I.

115 Go away from me, you sinful people.
    I will obey the commands of my God.
116 Give me strength, as you promised, and I
        shall live;
    don't let me be disappointed in my hope!
117 Hold me, and I will be safe,
        and I will always pay attention to your
        commands.
118 You reject everyone who disobeys your laws;
        their deceitful schemes are useless.
119 You treat all the wicked like rubbish,
        and so I love your instructions.
120 Because of you I am afraid;
        I am filled with fear because of your
        judgments.

Obedience to the Law of the Lord

121 I have done what is right and good;
        don't abandon me to my enemies!
122 Promise that you will help your servant;
        don't let the arrogant oppress me!
123 My eyes are tired from watching for your
        saving help,
    for the deliverance you promised.
124 Treat me according to your constant love,
        and teach me your commands.
125 I am your servant; give me understanding,
        so that I may know your teachings.
126 Lord, it is time for you to act,
        because people are disobeying your law.
127 I love your commands more than gold,
        more than the finest gold.

128 And so I follow all your instructions; *v*
    I hate all wrong ways.

Desire to Obey the Law of the LORD

129 Your teachings are wonderful;
    I obey them with all my heart.
130 The explanation of your teachings gives light
    and brings wisdom to the ignorant.
131 In my desire for your commands
    I pant with open mouth.
132 Turn to me and have mercy on me
    as you do on all those who love you.
133 As you have promised, keep me from falling;
    don't let me be overcome by evil.
134 Save me from those who oppress me,
    so that I may obey your commands.
135 Bless me with your presence
    and teach me your laws.
136 My tears pour down like a river,
    because people do not obey your law.

The Justice of the Law of the LORD

137 You are righteous, LORD,
    and your laws are just.
138 The rules that you have given
    are completely fair and right.
139 My anger burns in me like a fire,
    because my enemies disregard your
      commands.
140 How certain your promise is!
    How I love it!

v Some ancient translations all your instructions; *Hebrew unclear.*

¹⁴¹ I am unimportant and despised,
   but I do not neglect your teachings.
¹⁴² Your righteousness will last forever,
   and your law is always true.
¹⁴³ I am filled with trouble and anxiety,
   but your commandments bring me joy.
¹⁴⁴ Your instructions are always just;
   give me understanding, and I shall live.

A Prayer for Deliverance

¹⁴⁵ With all my heart I call to you;
   answer me, LORD, and I will obey your
      commands!
¹⁴⁶ I call to you;
   save me, and I will keep your laws.
¹⁴⁷ Before sunrise I call to you for help;
   I place my hope in your promise.
¹⁴⁸ All night long I lie awake,
   to meditate on your instructions.
¹⁴⁹ Because your love is constant, hear me,
      O LORD;
   show your mercy, and preserve my life!
¹⁵⁰ My cruel persecutors are coming closer,
   people who never keep your law.
¹⁵¹ But you are near to me, LORD,
   and all your commands are permanent.
¹⁵² Long ago I learned about your instructions;
   you made them to last forever.

A Plea for Help

¹⁵³ Look at my suffering, and save me,
   because I have not neglected your law.

154 Defend my cause, and set me free;
    save me, as you have promised.
155 The wicked will not be saved,
    for they do not obey your laws.
156 But your compassion, LORD, is great;
    show your mercy and save me!
157 I have many enemies and oppressors,
    but I do not fail to obey your laws.
158 When I look at those traitors, I am filled with
    disgust,
    because they do not keep your commands.
159 See how I love your instructions, LORD.
    Your love never changes, so save me!
160 The heart of your law is truth,
    and all your righteous judgments are
    eternal.

Dedication to the Law of the LORD

161 Powerful people attack me unjustly,
    but I respect your law.
162 How happy I am because of your promises—
    as happy as someone who finds rich
    treasure.
163 I hate and detest all lies,
    but I love your law.
164 Seven times each day I thank you
    for your righteous judgments.
165 Those who love your law have perfect
    security,
    and there is nothing that can make them
    fall.
166 I wait for you to save me, LORD,

and I do what you command.
¹⁶⁷ I obey your teachings;
    I love them with all my heart.
¹⁶⁸ I obey your commands and your instructions;
    you see everything I do.

A Prayer for Help

¹⁶⁹ Let my cry for help reach you, LORD!
    Give me understanding, as you have
        promised.
¹⁷⁰ Listen to my prayer,
    and save me according to your promise!
¹⁷¹ I will always praise you,
    because you teach me your laws.
¹⁷² I will sing about your law,
    because your commands are just.
¹⁷³ Always be ready to help me,
    because I follow your commands.
¹⁷⁴ How I long for your saving help, O LORD!
    I find happiness in your law.
¹⁷⁵ Give me life, so that I may praise you;
    may your instructions help me.
¹⁷⁶ I wander about like a lost sheep;
    so come and look for me, your servant,
    because I have not neglected your laws.

A Prayer for Help

120

When I was in trouble, I called to the
    LORD,
and he answered me.
² Save me, LORD,
    from liars and deceivers.

3 You liars, what will God do to you?
  How will he punish you?
4 With a soldier's sharp arrows,
  with red-hot coals!

5 Living among you is as bad as living in
    Meshech
  or among the people of Kedar.*w*
6 I have lived too long
  with people who hate peace!
7 When I speak of peace,
  they are for war.

The LORD Our Protector

121 I look to the mountains;
      where will my help come from?
2 My help will come from the LORD,
  who made heaven and earth.

3 He will not let you fall;
  your protector is always awake.

4 The protector of Israel
  never dozes or sleeps.
5 The LORD will guard you;
  he is by your side to protect you.
6 The sun will not hurt you during the day,
  nor the moon during the night.

w MESHECH . . . KEDAR: *Two distant regions, whose people were regarded as savages.*

7 The LORD will protect you from all danger;
    he will keep you safe.
8 He will protect you as you come and go
    now and forever.

In Praise of Jerusalem [x]

122 I was glad when they said to me,
        "Let us go to the LORD's house."
2 And now we are here,
    standing inside the gates of Jerusalem!

3 Jerusalem is a city restored
    in beautiful order and harmony.
4 This is where the tribes come,
    the tribes of Israel,
  to give thanks to the LORD
    according to his command.
5 Here the kings of Israel
    sat to judge their people.

6 Pray for the peace of Jerusalem:
    "May those who love you prosper.
7   May there be peace inside your walls
    and safety in your palaces."
8 For the sake of my relatives and friends
    I say to Jerusalem, "Peace be with you!"
9 For the sake of the house of the LORD
        our God
    I pray for your prosperity.

x HEBREW TITLE: *By David.*

A Prayer for Mercy

123 Lord, I look up to you,
  up to heaven, where you rule.
2 As a servant depends on his master,
  as a maid depends on her mistress,
so we will keep looking to you, O Lord
    our God,
  until you have mercy on us.

3 Be merciful to us, Lord, be merciful;
  we have been treated with so much
    contempt.
4 We have been mocked too long by the rich
  and scorned by proud oppressors.

God the Protector of His People *x*

124 What if the Lord had not been on our
    side?
  Answer, O Israel!

2 "If the Lord had not been on our side
  when our enemies attacked us,
3 then they would have swallowed us alive
  in their furious anger against us;
4 then the flood would have carried us away,
  the water would have covered us,
5   the raging torrent would have drowned us."

6 Let us thank the Lord,
  who has not let our enemies destroy us.

x HEBREW TITLE: *By David.*

7 We have escaped like a bird from a hunter's
      trap;
    the trap is broken, and we are free!
8 Our help comes from the LORD,
    who made heaven and earth.

The Security of God's People

125 Those who trust in the LORD are like
        Mount Zion,
    which can never be shaken, never be
      moved.
2 As the mountains surround Jerusalem,
    so the LORD surrounds his people,
    now and forever.

3 The wicked will not always rule over the land
    of the righteous;
    if they did, the righteous themselves might
    do evil.
4 LORD, do good to those who are good,
    to those who obey your commands.
5 But when you punish the wicked,
    punish also those who abandon your ways.

Peace be with Israel!

A Prayer for Deliverance

126 When the LORD brought us back to
        Jerusalem,[y]
    it was like a dream!
2 How we laughed, how we sang for joy!

[y] brought us back to Jerusalem; *or* made Jerusalem prosperous again.

Then the other nations said about us,
"The LORD did great things for them."
3 Indeed he did great things for us;
how happy we were!

4 LORD, make us prosperous again,[z]
just as the rain brings water back to dry
riverbeds.
5 Let those who wept as they planted their
crops,
gather the harvest with joy!

6 Those who wept as they went out carrying
the seed
will come back singing for joy,
as they bring in the harvest.

In Praise of God's Goodness [a]

127 If the LORD does not build the house,
the work of the builders is useless;
if the LORD does not protect the city,
it does no good for the sentries to stand
guard.
2 It is useless to work so hard for a living,
getting up early and going to bed late.
For the LORD provides for those he loves,
while they are asleep.

3 Children are a gift from the LORD;
they are a real blessing.
4 The sons a man has when he is young

[z] make us prosperous again; or take us back to our land.   [a] HEBREW TITLE: By
Solomon.

are like arrows in a soldier's hand.
5 Happy is the man who has many such arrows.
He will never be defeated
  when he meets his enemies in the place of
  judgment.

The Reward of Obedience to the LORD

128 Happy are those who obey the LORD,
    who live by his commands.

2 Your work will provide for your needs;
  you will be happy and prosperous.
3 Your wife will be like a fruitful vine in your
  home,
  and your children will be like young olive
  trees around your table.
4 A man who obeys the LORD
  will surely be blessed like this.

5 May the LORD bless you from Zion!
  May you see Jerusalem prosper
  all the days of your life!
6 May you live to see your grandchildren!

Peace be with Israel!

A Prayer against Israel's Enemies

129 Israel, tell us how your enemies have
    persecuted you
  ever since you were young.

2 "Ever since I was young,

> my enemies have persecuted me cruelly,
> but they have not overcome me.
> 3 They cut deep wounds in my back
> and made it like a plowed field.
> 4 But the LORD, the righteous one,
> has freed me from slavery."

> 5 May everyone who hates Zion
> be defeated and driven back.
> 6 May they all be like grass growing on the
> housetops,
> which dries up before it can grow;
> 7   no one gathers it up
> or carries it away in bundles.
> 8 No one who passes by will say,
> "May the LORD bless you!
> We bless you in the name of the LORD."

A Prayer for Help

130 From the depths of my despair I call to
you, LORD.
> 2 Hear my cry, O Lord;
> listen to my call for help!
> 3 If you kept a record of our sins,
> who could escape being condemned?
> 4 But you forgive us,
> so that we should stand in awe of you.

> 5 I wait eagerly for the LORD's help,
> and in his word I trust.
> 6 I wait for the Lord

more eagerly than sentries wait for the
    dawn—
than sentries wait for the dawn.

7 Israel, trust in the LORD,
    because his love is constant
    and he is always willing to save.
8 He will save his people Israel
    from all their sins.

A Prayer of Humble Trust [b]

131 LORD, I have given up my pride
    and turned away from my arrogance.
I am not concerned with great matters
    or with subjects too difficult for me.
2 Instead, I am content and at peace.
As a child lies quietly in its mother's arms,
    so my heart is quiet within me.
3 Israel, trust in the LORD
    now and forever!

In Praise of the Temple

132 LORD, do not forget David
    and all the hardships he endured.
2 Remember, LORD, what he promised,
    the vow he made to you, the Mighty God
    of Jacob:
3 "I will not go home or go to bed;
4   I will not rest or sleep,
5   until I provide a place for the LORD,
    a home for the Mighty God of Jacob."

b HEBREW TITLE: *By David.*

⁶ In Bethlehem we heard about the
     Covenant Box,
  and we found it in the fields of Jearim.
⁷ We said, "Let us go to the LORD's house;
  let us worship before his throne."

⁸ Come to the Temple, LORD, with the
     Covenant Box,
  the symbol of your power,
  and stay here forever.
⁹ May your priests do always what is right;
  may your people shout for joy!

¹⁰ You made a promise to your servant David;
  do not reject your chosen king, LORD.
¹¹ You made a solemn promise to David—
  a promise you will not take back:
  "I will make one of your sons king,
  and he will rule after you.
¹² If your sons are true to my covenant
  and to the commands I give them,
  their sons, also, will succeed you for all
     time as kings."

¹³ The LORD has chosen Zion;
  he wants to make it his home:
¹⁴ "This is where I will live forever;
  this is where I want to rule.
¹⁵ I will richly provide Zion with all she needs;
  I will satisfy her poor with food.
¹⁶ I will bless her priests in all they do,
  and her people will sing and shout for joy.

[17] Here I will make one of David's descendants
a great king;
here I will preserve the rule of my chosen
king.
[18] I will cover his enemies with shame,
but his kingdom will prosper and flourish."

In Praise of Living in Peace [b]

133 How wonderful it is, how pleasant,
for God's people to live together in
harmony!
[2] It is like the precious anointing oil
running down from Aaron's head and
beard,
down to the collar of his robes.
[3] It is like the dew on Mount Hermon,
falling on the hills of Zion.
That is where the LORD has promised his
blessing—
life that never ends.

A Call to Praise God

134 Come, praise the LORD,
all his servants,
all who serve in his Temple at night.
[2] Raise your hands in prayer in the Temple,
and praise the LORD!

[3] May the LORD, who made heaven and earth,
bless you from Zion!

[b] HEBREW TITLE: *By David.*

A Hymn of Praise

135 Praise the LORD!

Praise his name, you servants of the LORD,
2   who stand in the LORD's house,
   in the Temple of our God.
3 Praise the LORD, because he is good;
   sing praises to his name, because he is
     kind.*c*
4 He chose Jacob for himself,
   the people of Israel for his own.

5 I know that our LORD is great,
   greater than all the gods.
6 He does whatever he wishes
   in heaven and on earth,
   in the seas and in the depths below.
7 He brings storm clouds from the ends of the
     earth;
   he makes lightning for the storms,
   and he brings out the wind from his
     storeroom.

8 In Egypt he killed all the first-born
   of people and animals alike.
9 There he performed miracles and wonders
   to punish the king and all his officials.
10 He destroyed many nations
   and killed powerful kings:

c he is kind; *or* it is pleasant to do so.

11 Sihon, king of the Amorites,
  Og, king of Bashan,
  and all the kings in Canaan.
12 He gave their lands to his people;
  he gave them to Israel.

13 LORD, you will always be proclaimed as God;
  all generations will remember you.
14 The LORD will defend his people;
  he will take pity on his servants.

15 The gods of the nations are made of silver
    and gold;
  they are formed by human hands.
16 They have mouths, but cannot speak,
  and eyes, but cannot see.
17 They have ears, but cannot hear;
  they are not even able to breathe.
18 May all who made them and who trust in
    them
  become _d_ like the idols they have made!

19 Praise the LORD, people of Israel;
  praise him, you priests of God!
20 Praise the LORD, you Levites;
  praise him, all you that worship him!
21 Praise the LORD in Zion,
  in Jerusalem, his home.

  Praise the LORD!

_d_ May all . . . become; _or_ All who made them and who trust in them will become.

A Hymn of Thanksgiving

136 Give thanks to the LORD, because he is
good;
his love is eternal.
2 Give thanks to the greatest of all gods;
his love is eternal.
3 Give thanks to the mightiest of all lords;
his love is eternal.

4 He alone performs great miracles;
his love is eternal.
5 By his wisdom he made the heavens;
his love is eternal;
6 he built the earth on the deep waters;
his love is eternal.
7 He made the sun and the moon;
his love is eternal;
8 the sun to rule over the day;
his love is eternal;
9 the moon and the stars to rule over the night;
his love is eternal.

10 He killed the first-born sons of the Egyptians;
his love is eternal.
11 He led the people of Israel out of Egypt;
his love is eternal;
12 with his strong hand, his powerful arm;
his love is eternal.
13 He divided the Red Sea;
his love is eternal;

¹⁴ he led his people through it;
    his love is eternal;
¹⁵ but he drowned the king of Egypt and his
       army;
    his love is eternal.

¹⁶ He led his people through the desert;
    his love is eternal.
¹⁷ He killed powerful kings;
    his love is eternal;
¹⁸ he killed famous kings;
    his love is eternal;
¹⁹ Sihon, king of the Amorites;
    his love is eternal;
²⁰ and Og, king of Bashan;
    his love is eternal.
²¹ He gave their lands to his people;
    his love is eternal;
²² he gave them to Israel, his servant;
    his love is eternal.

²³ He did not forget us when we were defeated;
    his love is eternal;
²⁴ he freed us from our enemies;
    his love is eternal.
²⁵ He gives food to every living creature;
    his love is eternal.

²⁶ Give thanks to the God of heaven;
    his love is eternal.

A Lament of Israelites in Exile

137 By the rivers of Babylon we sat down;
there we wept when we remembered
Zion.

2 On the willows near by
we hung up our harps.

3 Those who captured us told us to sing;
they told us to entertain them:
"Sing us a song about Zion."

4 How can we sing a song to the LORD
in a foreign land?

5 May I never be able to play the harp again
if I forget you, Jerusalem!

6 May I never be able to sing again
if I do not remember you,
if I do not think of you as my greatest
joy!

7 Remember, LORD, what the Edomites did
the day Jerusalem was captured.
Remember how they kept saying,
"Tear it down to the ground!"

8 Babylon, you will be destroyed.
Happy are those who pay you back
for what you have done to us—

9   who take your babies
and smash them against a rock.

A Prayer of Thanksgiving [e]

138 I thank you, Lord, with all my heart;
 I sing praise to you before the gods.
2 I face your holy Temple,
 bow down, and praise your name
because of your constant love and
  faithfulness,
  because you have shown that your name
  and your commands are supreme. [f]
3 You answered me when I called to you;
 with your strength you strengthened me.

4 All the kings in the world will praise you,
  Lord,
  because they have heard your promises.
5 They will sing about what you have done
 and about your great glory.
6 Even though you are so high above,
 you care for the lowly,
 and the proud cannot hide from you.

7 When I am surrounded by troubles,
 you keep me safe.
 You oppose my angry enemies
 and save me by your power.
8 You will do everything you have promised;
 Lord, your love is eternal.
 Complete the work that you have begun.

[e] HEBREW TITLE: *By David.* [f] *Probable text* your name and your commands are supreme; *Hebrew* your command is greater than all your name.

God's Complete Knowledge and Care [g]

139 LORD, you have examined me and you
know me.

2 You know everything I do;
from far away you understand all my
thoughts.

3 You see me, whether I am working or resting;
you know all my actions.

4 Even before I speak,
you already know what I will say.

5 You are all around me on every side;
you protect me with your power.

6 Your knowledge of me is too deep;
it is beyond my understanding.

7 Where could I go to escape from you?
Where could I get away from your
presence?

8 If I went up to heaven, you would be there;
if I lay down in the world of the dead, you
would be there.

9 If I flew away beyond the east
or lived in the farthest place in the west,

10 you would be there to lead me,
you would be there to help me.

11 I could ask the darkness to hide me
or the light around me to turn into night,

12 but even darkness is not dark for you,
and the night is as bright as the day.
Darkness and light are the same to you.

[g] HEBREW TITLE: *A psalm by David.*

¹³ You created every part of me;
 you put me together in my mother's womb.
¹⁴ I praise you because you are to be feared;
 all you do is strange and wonderful.
 I know it with all my heart.
¹⁵ When my bones were being formed,
 carefully put together in my mother's
  womb,
when I was growing there in secret,
 you knew that I was there—
¹⁶ you saw me before I was born.
The days allotted to me
 had all been recorded in your book,
 before any of them ever began.
¹⁷ O God, how difficult I find your thoughts; ^h
 how many of them there are!
¹⁸ If I counted them, they would be more than
  the grains of sand.
 When I awake, I am still with you.

¹⁹ O God, how I wish you would kill the
  wicked!
 How I wish violent people would leave me
  alone!
²⁰ They say wicked things about you;
 they speak evil things against your name. ⁱ
²¹ O Lord, how I hate those who hate you!
 How I despise those who rebel against you!
²² I hate them with a total hatred;
 I regard them as my enemies.

^h how difficult I find your thoughts; *or* how precious are your thoughts to me.
ⁱ *Probable text* they speak . . . name; *Hebrew unclear.*

23 Examine me, O God, and know my mind;
    test me, and discover my thoughts.
24 Find out if there is any evil in me
    and guide me in the everlasting way.*j*

A Prayer for Protection *k*

140 Save me, LORD, from evildoers;
        keep me safe from violent people.
2 They are always plotting evil,
    always stirring up quarrels.
3 Their tongues are like deadly snakes;
    their words are like a cobra's poison.

4 Protect me, LORD, from the power of the
        wicked;
    keep me safe from violent people
    who plot my downfall.
5 The proud have set a trap for me;
    they have laid their snares,
    and along the path they have set traps to
        catch me.

6 I say to the LORD, "You are my God."
    Hear my cry for help, LORD!
7 My Sovereign LORD, my strong defender,
    you have protected me in battle.
8 LORD, don't give the wicked what they want;
    don't let their plots succeed.

9 Don't let my enemies be victorious;*l*

j the everlasting way; *or* the ways of my ancestors.   *k* HEBREW TITLE: *A psalm by David.*
l Probable text Don't let my enemies be victorious; *Hebrew unclear.*

make their threats against me fall back on
    them.
10 May red-hot coals fall on them;
    may they be thrown into a pit and never
    get out.
11 May those who accuse others falsely not
    succeed;
    may evil overtake violent people and
    destroy them.

12 LORD, I know that you defend the cause of
    the poor
    and the rights of the needy.
13 The righteous will praise you indeed;
    they will live in your presence.

An Evening Prayer [m]

141 I call to you, LORD; help me now!
    Listen to me when I call to you.
2 Receive my prayer as incense,
    my uplifted hands as an evening sacrifice.

3 LORD, place a guard at my mouth,
    a sentry at the door of my lips.
4 Keep me from wanting to do wrong
    and from joining evil people in their
    wickedness.
May I never take part in their feasts.

5 Good people may punish me and rebuke me
    in kindness,

[m] HEBREW TITLE: *A psalm by David.*

but I will never accept honor from evil
people,
because I am always praying against their
evil deeds.
6 When their rulers are thrown down from
rocky cliffs,
the people will admit that my words were
true.
7 Like wood that is split and chopped into bits,
so their bones are scattered at the edge of
the grave.[n]

8 But I keep trusting in you, my Sovereign
LORD.
I seek your protection;
don't let me die!
9 Protect me from the traps they have set
for me,
from the snares of those evildoers.
10 May the wicked fall into their own traps
while I go by unharmed.

A Prayer for Help [o]

142 I call to the LORD for help;
I plead with him.
2 I bring him all my complaints;
I tell him all my troubles.
3 When I am ready to give up,
he knows what I should do.
In the path where I walk,
my enemies have hidden a trap for me.

---

[n] *Verses 5-7 in Hebrew are unclear.*   [o] HEBREW TITLE: *A poem by David, when he was
in the cave; a prayer.*

4 When I look beside me,
    I see that there is no one to help me,
    no one to protect me.
  No one cares for me.

5 LORD, I cry to you for help;
    you, LORD, are my protector;
    you are all I want in this life.
6 Listen to my cry for help,
    for I am sunk in despair.
  Save me from my enemies;
    they are too strong for me.
7 Set me free from my distress; *p*
    then in the assembly of your people I will
      praise you
  because of your goodness to me.

A Prayer for Help *q*

143 LORD, hear my prayer!
    In your righteousness listen to my plea;
  answer me in your faithfulness!
2 Don't put me, your servant, on trial;
    no one is innocent in your sight.

3 My enemies have hunted me down
    and completely defeated me.
  They have put me in a dark prison,
    and I am like those who died long ago.

p distress; *or* prison.　　*q* HEBREW TITLE: *A psalm by David.*

⁴ So I am ready to give up;
  I am in deep despair.

⁵ I remember the days gone by;
  I think about all that you have done,
  I bring to mind all your deeds.
⁶ I lift up my hands to you in prayer;
  like dry ground my soul is thirsty for you.

⁷ Answer me now, LORD!
  I have lost all hope.
 Don't hide yourself from me,
  or I will be among those who go down to
    the world of the dead.
⁸ Remind me each morning of your constant
    love,
  for I put my trust in you.
 My prayers go up to you;
  show me the way I should go.

⁹ I go to you for protection, LORD;
  rescue me from my enemies.
¹⁰ You are my God;
  teach me to do your will.
 Be good to me, and guide me on a safe path.

¹¹ Rescue me, LORD, as you have promised;
  in your goodness save me from my
    troubles!
¹² Because of your love for me, kill my enemies
  and destroy all my oppressors,
  for I am your servant.

A King Thanks God for Victory[r]

144 Praise the LORD, my protector!
He trains me for battle
and prepares me for war.
2 He is my protector and defender,
my shelter and savior,
in whom I trust for safety.
He subdues the nations under me.

3 LORD, what are mortals, that you notice them;
mere mortals, that you pay attention to us?
4 We are like a puff of wind;
our days are like a passing shadow.

5 O LORD, tear the sky open and come down;
touch the mountains, and they will pour out
smoke.
6 Send flashes of lightning and scatter your
enemies;
shoot your arrows and send them running.
7 Reach down from above,
pull me out of the deep water, and
rescue me;
save me from the power of foreigners,
8   who never tell the truth
and lie even under oath.

9 I will sing you a new song, O God;
I will play the harp and sing to you.
10 You give victory to kings
and rescue your servant David.

r HEBREW TITLE: *By David.*

11 Save me from my cruel enemies;
   rescue me from the power of foreigners,
   who never tell the truth
   and lie even under oath.

12 May our sons in their youth
   be like plants that grow up strong.
May our daughters be like stately columns
   which adorn the corners of a palace.
13 May our barns be filled
   with crops of every kind.
May the sheep in our fields
   bear young by the tens of thousands.
14 May our cattle reproduce plentifully
   without miscarriage or loss.
May there be no cries of distress in our
   streets.

15 Happy is the nation of whom this is true;
   happy are the people whose God is the
   LORD!

A Hymn of Praise [s]

145   I will proclaim your greatness, my God
       and king;
   I will thank you forever and ever.
2 Every day I will thank you;
   I will praise you forever and ever.
3 The LORD is great and is to be highly praised;
   his greatness is beyond understanding.

s HEBREW TITLE: *A song of praise by David.*

4 What you have done will be praised from one
generation to the next;
they will proclaim your mighty acts.
5 They will speak of your glory and majesty,
and I will meditate on your wonderful
deeds.
6 People will speak of your mighty deeds,
and I will proclaim your greatness.
7 They will tell about all your goodness
and sing about your kindness.
8 The Lord is loving and merciful,
slow to become angry and full of constant
love.
9 He is good to everyone
and has compassion on all he made.

10 All your creatures, Lord, will praise you,
and all your people will give you thanks.
11 They will speak of the glory of your royal
power
and tell of your might,
12 so that everyone will know your mighty deeds
and the glorious majesty of your kingdom.
13 Your rule is eternal,
and you are king forever.

The Lord is faithful to his promises;
he is merciful in all his acts.
14 He helps those who are in trouble;
he lifts those who have fallen.

15 All living things look hopefully to you,
and you give them food when they need it.

16 You give them enough
  and satisfy the needs of all.

17 The LORD is righteous in all he does,
  merciful in all his acts.
18 He is near to those who call to him,
  who call to him with sincerity.
19 He supplies the needs of those who
      honor him;
  he hears their cries and saves them.
20 He protects everyone who loves him,
  but he will destroy the wicked.

21 I will always praise the LORD;
  let all his creatures praise his holy name
    forever.

In Praise of God the Savior

146 Praise the LORD!
  Praise the LORD, my soul!
2 I will praise him as long as I live;
  I will sing to my God all my life.

3 Don't put your trust in human leaders;
  no human being can save you.
4 When they die, they return to the dust;
  on that day all their plans come to an end.

5 Happy are those who have the God of Jacob
      to help them
  and who depend on the LORD their God,
6   the Creator of heaven, earth, and sea,

and all that is in them.
He always keeps his promises;
7   he judges in favor of the oppressed
and gives food to the hungry.

The LORD sets prisoners free
8   and gives sight to the blind.
He lifts those who have fallen;
he loves his righteous people.
9 He protects the strangers who live in our
land;
he helps widows and orphans,
but takes the wicked to their ruin.

10 The LORD is king forever.
Your God, O Zion, will reign for all time.

Praise the LORD!

In Praise of God the Almighty

147 Praise the LORD!

It is good to sing praise to our God;
it is pleasant and right to praise him.
2 The LORD is restoring Jerusalem;
he is bringing back the exiles.
3 He heals the broken-hearted
and bandages their wounds.

4 He has decided the number of the stars
and calls each one by name.
5 Great and mighty is our Lord;

his wisdom cannot be measured.
6 He raises the humble,
    but crushes the wicked to the ground.

7 Sing hymns of praise to the LORD;
    play music on the harp to our God.
8 He spreads clouds over the sky;
    he provides rain for the earth
    and makes grass grow on the hills.
9 He gives animals their food
    and feeds the young ravens when they call.

10 His pleasure is not in strong horses,
    nor his delight in brave soldiers;
11 but he takes pleasure in those who honor him,
    in those who trust in his constant love.

12 Praise the LORD, O Jerusalem!
    Praise your God, O Zion!
13 He keeps your gates strong;
    he blesses your people.
14 He keeps your borders safe
    and satisfies you with the finest wheat.

15 He gives a command to the earth,
    and what he says is quickly done.
16 He spreads snow like a blanket
    and scatters frost like dust.
17 He sends hail like gravel;
    no one can endure the cold he sends!
18 Then he gives a command, and the ice melts;
    he sends the wind, and the water flows.

¹⁹ He gives his message to his people,
    his instructions and laws to Israel.
²⁰ He has not done this for other nations;
    they do not know his laws.

Praise the LORD!

A Call for the Universe to Praise God

148   Praise the LORD!

Praise the LORD from heaven,
    you that live in the heights above.
² Praise him, all his angels,
    all his heavenly armies.

³ Praise him, sun and moon;
    praise him, shining stars.
⁴ Praise him, highest heavens,
    and the waters above the sky.ᵗ

⁵ Let them all praise the name of the LORD!
He commanded, and they were created;
⁶   by his command they were fixed in their
    places forever,
    and they cannot disobey.ᵘ

⁷ Praise the LORD from the earth,
    sea monsters and all ocean depths;
⁸ lightning and hail, snow and clouds,
    strong winds that obey his command.

ᵗ WATERS ABOVE THE SKY: *See Gn 1.6, 7.*   ᵘ by his command . . . disobey; *or* he has fixed
them in their places for all time, by a command that lasts forever.

9 Praise him, hills and mountains,
   fruit trees and forests;
10 all animals, tame and wild,
   reptiles and birds.

11 Praise him, kings and all peoples,
   princes and all other rulers;
12 young women and young men,
   old people and children too.

13 Let them all praise the name of the LORD!
   His name is greater than all others;
      his glory is above earth and heaven.
14 He made his nation strong,
   so that all his people praise him—
   the people of Israel, so dear to him.

Praise the LORD!

A Hymn of Praise

149   Praise the LORD!

Sing a new song to the LORD;
   praise him in the assembly of his faithful
      people!
2 Be glad, Israel, because of your Creator;
   rejoice, people of Zion, because of your
      king!
3 Praise his name with dancing;
   play drums and harps in praise of him.

4 The LORD takes pleasure in his people;

he honors the humble with victory.
5 Let God's people rejoice in their triumph
   and sing joyfully all night long.
6 Let them shout aloud as they praise God,
   with their sharp swords in their hands
7   to defeat the nations
   and to punish the peoples;
8   to bind their kings in chains,
   their leaders in chains of iron;
9   to punish the nations as God has
     commanded.
This is the victory of God's people.

Praise the LORD!

Praise the LORD!

150   Praise the LORD!

Praise God in his Temple!
   Praise his strength in heaven!
2 Praise him for the mighty things he has done.
   Praise his supreme greatness.

3 Praise him with trumpets.
   Praise him with harps and lyres.
4 Praise him with drums and dancing.
   Praise him with harps and flutes.
5 Praise him with cymbals.
   Praise him with loud cymbals.
6 Praise the LORD, all living creatures!

Praise the LORD!

ONE COMPELLING PURPOSE

"The Bible in the language of the people" is the guiding spirit behind the ministry of the American Bible Society. The entire program of the Society can be summed up in the one compelling purpose of making the Holy Scriptures readily available to all people throughout the world in languages which they clearly understand and at prices which they can easily afford. This inexpensive Bible in the clear and accurate language of the *Today's English Version* and with non-doctrinal aids for the reader is an example of what the Bible Society is doing throughout the world in hundreds of languages to make the Word of God more easily available to all.

The Bible Society program of translating the Bible into the living language of everyday use in hundreds of languages is growing each year. In addition, in most countries and languages the actual distribution of the Bible must be heavily subsidized if it is to be within the reach of most people.

No task in the in the world is more important than reaching every person on earth with the Word of God. In order to accomplish this goal, the American Bible Society, together with its dedicated Bible Society partners around the world, has created an efficient organization based on almost two centuries of experience in providing the Holy Scriptures in the languages of more than 90 percent of the world's population.

For information about how you can help meet this world need for the Word of God, write:

American Bible Society
1865 Broadway
New York, N.Y. 10023